The Flowing River of Dharma

Also by Anyen Rinpoche and Allison Choying Zangmo

Stop Biting the Tail You're Chasing
The Tibetan Yoga of Breath

Also by Anyen Rinpoche

The Union of Dzogchen and Bodhichitta
Dying with Confidence
Journey to Certainty
Momentary Buddhism

Also by Allison Choying Zangmo

The Guide to Enlightenment

The Flowing River of Dharma

Instructions on *Parting from the Four Attachments*

Featuring Sakya, Kagyu, Nyingma,
Kadam of Old, and Gelug Teachings

ANYEN RINPOCHE AND
ALLISON CHOYING ZANGMO

Foreword by His Holiness the Gongma Trichen

SHAMBHALA

Shambhala Publications, Inc.
2129 13th Street
Boulder, Colorado 80302
www.shambhala.com

Copyright © 2025 by Anyen Rinpoche and Allison Choying Zangmo

Unless attributed, all quotes are translations from Tibetan sources or are from Rinpoche's oral teachings.

Cover art: bombomtea/stock.adobe.com
Cover design: Kate E. White

All rights reserved. No part of this book may be reproduced in any form or by any means, electronic or mechanical, including photocopying, recording, or by any information storage and retrieval system, without permission in writing from the publisher.

9 8 7 6 5 4 3 2 1

First Edition
Printed in the United States of America

Shambhala Publications makes every effort to print on acid-free, recycled paper.
Shambhala Publications is distributed worldwide by Penguin Random House, Inc., and its subsidiaries.

LIBRARY OF CONGRESS CATALOGING-IN-PUBLICATION DATA
Names: Anyen, Rinpoche, author. | Zangmo, Allison Choying, author.
Title: The flowing river of dharma: instructions on parting from the four attachments featuring Sakya, Kagyu, Nyingma, Kadam of old, and Gelug teachings / Anyen Rinpoche and Allison Choying Zangmo.
Description: First edition. | Boulder, Colorado: Shambhala, [2025] |
Identifiers: LCCN 2024060347 | ISBN 9781645473626 (trade paperback)
Subjects: LCSH: Dharma (Buddhism) | Sa-skya-pa (Sect)—Doctrines. | Bka'-brgyud-pa (Sect)—Doctrines. | Rnying-ma-pa (Sect)—Doctrines. | Bka'-gdams-pa (Sect)—Doctrines. | Dge-lugs-pa (Sect)—Doctrines.
Classification: LCC BQ4190 .A594 2025 | DDC 294.3—dc23/eng/20250303
LC record available at https://lccn.loc.gov/2024060347

The authorized representative in the EU for product safety and compliance is eucomply OÜ, Pärnu mnt 139b-14, 11317 Tallinn, Estonia, hello@eucompliancepartner.com.

For all the authentic masters of the Vajrayana and all who aspire to follow in their footsteps.

Tsara Dharmakirti Rinpoche

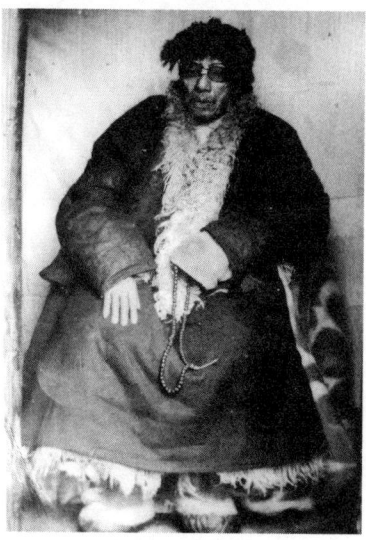

Lama Tsepel

The Four Dharma Traditions of the Land of Tibet

By Mipham Rinpoche

Nyingma practitioners emphasize the meaning of the tantric
  treatises.
They pursue the highest view and delight in unpredictable
  conduct.
Many reach the level of a Vidyadhara and attain
  accomplishment,
And many are Ngakpas, whose power is greater than others.

Kagyu practitioners, refuge of beings, emphasize faith and
  devotion.
Many mature based on the lineage blessings,
And many attain accomplishment through persevering in
  hardship.
They are similar to, and mingle with, the Nyingmapas.

The glorious Sakyapas emphasize the recitation of mantra and
  sadhanas.
Many are blessed through the power of their visualization and
  recitation.

They value their own tradition, and their daily practice is
uninterrupted.
They have some of the qualities of each of the other schools.

The Riwo Gendenpas emphasize the scholarly tradition.
They enjoy analytical meditation and delight in debate,
And they impress everyone with their elegant, exemplary
conduct.
They have many followers, are prosperous, and make effort at
studying.

Ema! All four dharma traditions of this land of Tibet
Have but one actual source, even though they appeared
individually.
Whichever one you follow—if you practice it properly—
It will bring the qualities of learning and accomplishment.

So, like children of the same father and the same mother,
Cultivate harmony, devotion, and pure perception,
And, while focusing on your own tradition, avoid belittling
others.
Acting in this way, you will also serve the dharma.

I, Mipham, wrote this on the thirtieth day of the first month of
the fire-monkey year (1896). *Mangalam!*

Contents

༄༅། །དེ་ཡང་གཞུང་དང་མན་ངག་གི་ཆོས་ཚུལ་རྗེ་སྤྲུད་ཅིག་བཞུགས་པ་ལས། རྗེ་བཙུན་འཇམ་པའི་དབྱངས་ཀྱི་ཞལ་སྔ་ནས་བླ་མ་ས་སྐྱ་པ་ཆེན་པོ་ལ་བསྐུལ་བའི་བློ་སྦྱོང་ཞེན་པ་བཞི་བྲལ་ཏེ། མཚན་གྱི་ཆ་ནས་བློ་སྦྱོང་སྦྱོང་འགྲོའི་ཆོས་སྐོར་ཞེས་ལུ་ཞིང་། དོན་གྱི་ཆ་ནས་མདོ་རྒྱུད་ས་ལུས་པའི་དོན་གྱི་བཅུད་ཕྱུང་བའི་མན་ངག་ཀུན་གྱི་སྙིང་པོ་འདི་བཞིན་ད་ལམ་ལ་སྐྱུན་རིན་པོ་ཆེ་མཆོག་དང་ཆོས་དབྱིངས་བཟང་མོ་གཉིས་ནས་དབྱིན་སྐད་དུ་བསྒྱུར་ཅིང་ལུས་ཏེ་དཔར་བསྐྲུན་གནང་ང་ལ་རྗེ་སུ་ཡི་རང་དང་བསྔགས་བརྗོད་ཞུ་བ་སྒྲགས། གདམས་པ་འདི་འང་ང་བ་བླ་མ་ས་སྐྱ་པ་ཆེན་པོར་བཀའ་བབ་པའི་ཞེན་པ་བཞི་བྲལ་གཞིར་བྱས་ཕོག འབགས་པོ་བློ་སྦྱོང་གི་ལམ་སློལ་རྩ་མེད་པ་སྒྲོགས་གཅིག་ཏུ་བསྟེབས་ཅིང་། བ་པད་སྐྲུབ་འཆུན་ཉན་དང་ཕྱིན་རྣམས་བཀྲུབ་པ་བར་མ་ཆད་ད་བཞུགས་པ་ལ་རྗེ་བཙུན་རིན་པོ་ཆེ་གྲགས་པ་རྒྱལ་མཚན་གྱིས་མཛད་པ་འདི་བཞིན་སྐྱར་གྱི་བྱ་ཐབས་དོན་སྐུར་ཐད་བསྐུར་གྱིས་མཆེན་པ་རིགས་ཀྱི་ག་ཁྲལ་ལ་ཐེམ་པའི་ཕྱུ་བཞིས་སྐོམ་གཞིར་བཀུན་པའི་ཕོག དེང་རབས་སྐྲ་ཡིག་རིགས་པའི་བགྲོས་དང་མཐུན་པར་བསྐུར་གཞང་ཡོད་པར་གོར་མ་ཆག་ན། གདམས་པ་འདི་ལ་བརྟེན་ནས་སྐྱལ་བ་ཕྱུན་པའི་གང་ཟག་རྣམས་བློ་སྦྱོང་ཐབ་མོས་རྒྱུད་ཕྲུལ་པ་དང་། འདི་ཕྱུར་བགྱིས་པའི་རྣམ་དཀར་དགེ་བས་རིགས་དྲུག་བར་དོ་དང་བཅས་པའི་འགྲོ་བ་མ་ལུས་པ་དལ་རྟེན་རིན་བཀུན། ཚོགས་གཉིས་སྙུར་དུ་རྫོགས་ནས་བྱུང་འཛུག་རྒྱལ་བ་རྡོ་རྗེ་འཆང་ཆེན་པོའི་གོ་འཕང་ལ་རེགས་པའི་སྐྱབས་སྐྱོན་ཐྱེད། འཕགས་ཡུལ་རྡ་ཛ་པུར་ནས། ས་སྐྱ་ཁྲི་ཆེན་པས། ཕྱི་ལོ་ ༢༠༢༥ ཟླ་ ཚེས་ ༢༡ དགེ་བ་ལ། །

Foreword

Parting from the Four Attachments was received by the great Sakya Lama [Drakpa Gyaltsen] directly from the mouth of Jetsun Manjushri. It is included in both the textual tradition and upadesha instructions that convey the dharma. From the point of view of its title, it is known as the *Cycle of the Preliminary Practice of Lojong*. From the point of view of its meaning, it extracts the essence of the sutra and tantra in its entirety and contains the heart of all upadesha instructions. As such, I praise and rejoice in the publishing of this book, written in English by Anyen Rinpoche and Allison Choying Zangmo.

This book's main topics are the holder of this sacred teaching, the Great Sakya Lama, and the unblemished, unified tradition of lojong from India and Tibet. It includes a translation of the teachings as well as the meaning of the uninterrupted lineage of teaching and practice, explanation and listening, and blessings originating in Jetsun Rinpoche Drakpa Gyaltsen. This ornament—the vast casket [of lojong teachings] that has become part of the Tibetan people's very flesh and blood—has been unequivocally written for a modern audience, using words and explanations they can understand.

May this book enrich the minds of fortunate beings with the profound lojong teachings and, by any completely pure virtue accumulated by its composition, may migrating beings of the six classes and in the bardos—without exception—attain a precious human life from lifetime to lifetime. After quickly perfecting the two accumulations, may they reach the state of the indivisible monarch, the great Vajradhara.

—His Holiness the Gongma Trichen
  Rajpur, India
  August 21, 2025

PART ONE

Introducing the Rime Style of Teaching and Practice

My root lama, Tsara Dharmakirti Rinpoche, painstakingly ensured that I understood what it meant to be a genuine practitioner of the dharma—a person disciplined in practice with a heart devoted to the well-being of others, but also someone with little attachment to myself, my own status, and worldly life. The pages that follow share an essential teaching of the dharma—*Parting from the Four Attachments*—in a way that he often used to introduce ideas from Vajrayana Buddhism.

While Tsara Dharmakirti Rinpoche's teachings often focused on the words of Longchen Nyingthig masters such as Longchen Rabjam, Jigme Lingpa, Patrul Rinpoche, and others, his instruction was unique in that it interwove the words and wisdom of two succinct and seemingly simple quotations from two Tibetan Buddhist masters—one from the Sakya tradition, and the other from the Kagyu tradition. Of course, he also relied heavily on the words of Longchen Nyingthig masters as he gave these teachings, which enabled him to illustrate how these masters agreed on their approach to and realization of the Vajrayana.

The first verse he shared, *Parting from the Four Attachments*, is by the famous Sakya master Sakya Drakpa Gyaltsen. It comprises the main part of the teaching and is also the main topic of this book.

If you are attached to this life, you are not a dharma
   practitioner.
If you are attached to samsara, you do not have
   renunciation.
If you are attached to self-interest, you do not have
   bodhicitta.
If any grasping is present, it is not the view.

Sakya Drakpa Gyaltsen's verse distills the very essence of the
dharma into four lines. It is incredibly useful to have the chance
to study a profound verse like this in detail, in the manner introduced in this book. As dharma practitioners with limited knowledge, wisdom, and lifespans, we don't have enough time to receive
teachings on the entirety of the sutra and tantra and practice them
completely. It is difficult to retain what we learn and to synthesize
a presentation with many elaborate points into something that is
succinct and easy to practice.

Because the so-called oceanic dharma is so vast and difficult
to master, there is a style of teaching in the Vajrayana called *upadesha.* Upadesha teachings are brief, they express the key points
of the dharma, and they capture a profound meaning that can
enable a practitioner to achieve unerring and swift realization.
Practitioners of the Nyingma school, like myself, associate the
word *upadesha* with the tradition of the innermost secret heart
essence of the Longchen Nyingthig—the teachings of Atiyoga Dzogchen. But within the tradition of *lojong,* or mind training, there
are also upadesha-style teachings that point out and teach how
to take up the conduct and path of a bodhisattva in a succinct
and profound way.

Upadesha instructions are passed down through an oral lineage from master to student and are practiced just as taught.
Once a student achieves realization of the instructions, they

pass on the teachings to other qualified students. This creates a lineage of the teachings, whereby these pithy and profound messages retain their pristine quality. *Parting from the Four Attachments* belongs to the category of upadesha because it condenses the entire meaning of the sutra and tantra into one verse. You will see what this means as you read the pages of this book—if you are able to gain a deep understanding of the scope and meaning of these four lines, your practice and path of dharma will be unerring. Because the meaning of *Parting from the Four Attachments* places us firmly on the path and ensures that we don't stray from the main points until we reach complete liberation, this verse is well known among genuine practitioners in Tibet. No matter what lineage they practice—Gelug, Sakya, Kagyu, or Nyingma—they accept this verse as an expression of unmistaken, profound dharma.

As you can imagine, a commentary on its meaning could be extremely vast or quite succinct, depending on the master giving the teachings. This book includes both—an elaborate explanation and a concise one. The extensive explanation will be given according to the teachings of Tsara Dharmakirti Rinpoche. But my lama also sent me to receive teachings on this verse from Lama Tsepel, a lifelong retreatant and hermit. Lama Tsepel's instructions were transmitted to me with very few words. Despite their brevity, his teachings had an immense impact on me. I would even say they thoroughly changed my approach to the dharma and caused me to look deeply inward at my own good qualities and faults as a practitioner.

The second verse my lama relied upon when he gave this commentary is *The Four Dharmas of Gampopa*. This verse is used to support Sakya Drakpa Gyaltsen's verse and follows along naturally with its meaning.

Grant your blessing so that my mind may turn toward the
dharma.
Grant your blessing so that dharma may progress along the
path.
Grant your blessing so that the path may clarify confusion.
Grant your blessing so that confusion may dawn as wisdom.

Why would a well-known Longchen Nyingthig scholar from
Shri Singha Shedra at Dzogchen Monastery choose to introduce
the Vajrayana by relying on the words of masters from other lineages? This is typical of the *rime* (often translated as "nonsectarian") movement, and Tsara Dharmakirti Rinpoche was considered
a rime master in Tibet. He had students from all four lineages
of Tibetan Buddhism, as well as students from the Bon tradition—and even more surprising, one of his closest students and
my closest dharma brothers at the *shedra* was from the Sakya
lineage. Because of his rime approach to study and practice, Tsara
Dharmakirti Rinpoche could teach any student in just the way
they needed, giving them the teachings from their own lineage or
teachings based on a combination of mutually supportive verses
and texts, as is contained in this book.

What Is Rime?

The rime movement was started in Tibet in the nineteenth century
by the renowned Nyingma master Jamyang Khyentse Wangpo.
A beautiful approach, rime views the wisdom of all lineages as
equal and complementary. Practitioners of the rime style don't
think of the teachings of their lineage as superior to others. Rather,
they view the other lineages and sects of Vajrayana Buddhism as
different paths to the same realization. This lessens the tendency
to look down on what others study and practice, and it increases
interest in the study and practice of the teachings of other lineages.

As a result of the rime movement, many Tibetan lineages have flourished and spread throughout Tibet and beyond, ensuring these teachings and practices will endure longer. The Dalai Lama actively follows the rime approach to study and practice, both as a support to his own practice and to increase cooperation and harmony between different Vajrayana lineages and schools, which ultimately makes their teachings stronger and more enduring.

Especially in modern times and among practitioners who were raised in and live in democratic nations, the rime approach resonates with many people. Those who value democratic values such as fairness, justice, and equality may feel that the rime approach is exactly how modern Vajrayana should be practiced. As a result, we may avoid committing to one lama, one lineage, or one school of the Vajrayana in a serious way. We may feel that making a serious commitment to a particular teacher, lineage, or school diminishes our connection to the Vajrayana—for example, if we focused too heavily on one approach, we worry we would become like a one-eyed yak who can only see the grass on our left and not our right. Or we might also have the idea that because the wisdom of the lineage masters is one and the same, that we can mix them and practice them indiscriminately as was seemingly done by great rime masters of the past, such as Jamyang Khyentse Wangpo, Jamgon Kongtrul, and Patrul Rinpoche.

Modern practitioners of the Vajrayana often describe themselves as rime, perhaps without knowing the genuine meaning of that word. The word *rime* isn't synonymous with simply seeing the lineages, schools, or even practices of the dharma as essentially the same such that they can be recombined in any possible way with no need for the organization or transmission of a lineage. For example, we may have the thought that because all Vajrayana masters possess wisdom, that everything they teach is the same or "one." However, the rime approach is not exactly egalitarian. It relies on a deep commitment and realization of one lineage of teachings, which enables one to see the complementary and mutually supportive teachings of other traditions.

This idea of singularity or oneness is very popular with modern practitioners. The indivisible state of singularity or oneness is something described by the Vajrayana on an ultimate level—but these teachings can't be applied to ordinary phenomena in the way that is being suggested. After all, if all the teachings are the same, why did anyone bother articulating them differently? There must be some use in the differences and great variety of lineage teachings and methods found in the Vajrayana.

Even the common translation of *rime* as "nonsectarian" doesn't do the word justice, as this word implies that one might not even practice the teachings of a single lineage or school of the Vajrayana. For example, we might receive all kinds of Vajrayana teachings from the various schools and then take some of them and put them together to create our own personal practice. In Tibet, we say, "Don't mix the teachings together like *tsampa* and cheese."* I have often heard about this kind of approach being taken by modern practitioners who feel empowered, independent, or self-directed in their study of the dharma. I have met many people who follow this way of thinking, treating the Vajrayana more like a college catalog, where they select courses of interest and design their own education.

But do you really know what the essential elements of dharma practice are? How can you be sure that the teachings and practices you choose will create the positive conditions for spiritual progress and transformation? You may have misunderstood the reason for such a variety of practice lineages and teachings in the Vajrayana. These distinct lineages, with distinct teachings and practice traditions, are available for the benefit of the very different

---

* Tsampa is barley flour, traditionally eaten by Tibetans as a cereal or dough. The phrase means to not try to make two things that are not like each other seem like they are the same.

dispositions of individual practitioners. The lineages of Vajrayana Buddhism were either arranged or revealed (in the case of *termas**) by realized masters. But because you aren't fully educated in the Vajrayana and you lack the realization of the great masters, you may not even realize that the way you are practicing won't help you make much progress.

Based on taking up various practices of our own design, we may notice some changes in the beginning. However, those changes may not continue to grow and deepen. The realization of the Vajrayana path is the result of very specific essential elements, skills, and teachings that are presented within the teachings of a particular lineage. If we practice in an unsystematic way, even if we are very committed to the dharma, sooner or later we may give up practicing when we don't achieve the result we expect—or, at the very least, our progress doesn't meet our expectations. For this reason, Vajrayana masters advocate following the teachings of a lineage fully and following the guidance of a qualified master who can help us to avoid these pitfalls and guide us through the process of spiritual maturation.

A more full and correct understanding of the meaning of rime can be described in this way: viewing the essential meaning of the Gelugpa, Sakya, Kagyu, and Nyingma teachings, as well as the teachings of the nine vehicles† as a whole, as streams that converge into a single river and flow under one bridge. The crucial question: How does a practitioner go about bringing these separate streams under the same bridge? I would answer that by saying that when a master has achieved a high state of realization through the teachings

---

* Termas are teachings that were hidden principally by Padmasambhava and rediscovered by later karmically connected lineage masters when the time was ripe to share the teachings.

† The nine vehcies are: the Shravaka, Prateykabuddha, and Mahayana; the three outer tantric vehicles (the Kriya, Upa, and Yoga Tantras), and the three inner tantric vehicles (Mahayoga, Anuyoga, and Atiyoga).

of one lineage, their wisdom penetrates the meaning of every dharma teaching they read. They are able to see and realize the intended wisdom and meaning of it all. In other words, because they gain a deep realization of the view, meditation, and conduct of their main practice lineage, they are able to kindle unbiased and impartial devotion and pure perception toward the teachings of the buddhadharma as a whole.

I would again point out that this goes beyond a mere intellectual approach—although having an intellectual approach is also a great asset for any dharma practitioner, as long as they are committed to a qualified lama and a particular lineage. This is because a rime practitioner must first commit to practicing the teachings of a single lineage and gain at least some realization of that lineage. Then when they examine the meaning of the teachings of the other Vajrayana schools, they will see that all of them present teachings on pure view, meditation, and conduct that can lead a practitioner to complete realization. This kind of determination enables a master to realize (based on wisdom, not intellect) that the meaning of all these teachings is uncontradictory.

I would like to point out that the realization of the singular wisdom of the Vajrayana doesn't only apply to the meaning of the tantras. It refers to the buddhadharma, the entirety of the nine vehicles. For example, a rime master like my root lama would read the *Heart Sutra* as expressing the meaning of Atiyoga Dzogchen due to his own realization of the teachings as being mutually supportive and uncontradictory, rather than simply a commentary asserting the emptiness of all phenomena.

Je Tsongkapa's Explanation of Rime

Although not a rime master himself, the renowned Gelugpa scholar Je Tsongkapa laid the foundation for the rime tradition in his teachings. He described a rime master as having the following four qualities: (1) the great vision that sees all of the teachings of the sutra and tantra as practical instructions; (2) the great wisdom to understand the philosophy of the four schools of Vajrayana as being free of contradiction; (3) the great ease in realizing the meaning of the profound primordial wisdom and wisdom intent of the Vajrayana as a whole; and (4) the great quality of cutting through and pacifying all afflictive emotions naturally.

As for the first quality, because of a rime master's deep realization of their own lineage teachings, no matter what teaching they reflect upon, that teaching will appear in the mind of the master as practical instructions to liberate the mind from afflictive emotions. This occurs because all mind-training methods in the Vajrayana are seen and used in a harmonious manner, and this way of seeing is incredibly effective at purifying the mind of its negative habits and tendencies.

This is not the case for ordinary practitioners. When ordinary practitioners read a particular text, it appears to us to be of a certain level or a certain style. Even if we consider ourselves to be very broad-minded, we still have biases and preferences. We may think certain teachings are more profound than others. Or we may prefer to receive teachings, transmissions, or practices that we think are of a *higher level*. On a practical level, we may not be as motivated to practice teachings from the general sutra or Mahayana as we are to practice teachings at the level of Atiyoga Dzogchen. When we read the texts of different Vajrayana schools, we may prefer to read a text on Secret Mantra rather than something from the Gelupga, Sakya, or Kagyu schools. But this is not the case for a rime master. A rime master genuinely experiences the entire buddhadharma as a cohesive whole and all these expositions of the dharma as part of the same set of methods and realization. There is no need to prefer one to another, thinking one is more profound than another, because all of them can be equally used to enhance the experience of realization.

We could also come from the completely opposite point of view—that of being so attached to the particular lineage or school of Buddhism we practice that we can't see the good qualities of the others at all. In this case, we can't even entertain the idea of rime at all, since we see our own practice, lineage, or lama as superior. This enhances one of the special qualities of a rime practitioner: having a strong sense of pure perception and respect for all Buddhist lineages, schools, and masters. This type of pure vision toward the teachings makes it much easier for a rime master to see the teachings of the sutra and tantra as practical instructions.

The second quality is to see the philosophies of the four schools as being free of contradiction. Vajrayana Buddhism is known for its scholarly debate about the conventional and ultimate nature of phenomena. There is a great amount of disagreement between the scholars of the different schools who debate back and forth to clarify and prove which school's point of view is more elevated or profound. Ordinarily a master of one lineage will take the position of their own school's philosophy and see the view of other schools as less refined. This style of debate is used to help Buddhist scholars sharpen their understanding and conviction in the philosophy and teachings of their own school. But in this case, the view, meditation, and conduct of each school are all realized as equal in being a perfectly pure path to achieving the state of twofold omniscient wisdom,* or buddhahood.

The third quality—that of ease in realizing the profound meaning of the buddhadharma—is a direct result of having realized the first two. It is almost as though the entirety of the buddhadharma has been distilled into a tonic that can be digested so that realization of the teachings dawns almost effortlessly. In this case, the dharma can be fully applied because not a single teaching or

---

* The state of twofold omniscient wisdom refers to omniscience with regard to both conventional and ultimate reality.

method is left out. Everything can be applied using the lens of that master's realization and embracing of the view, meditation, and conduct of all four schools of the Vajrayana. The result of this quality is that the master is easily released from the bonds of self-attachment.

Finally, the fourth quality—naturally pacifying the afflictive emotions—occurs once our self-attachment has been fully eradicated as a result of fully internalizing and actualizing the meaning of the buddhadharma, as described in the first three qualities. Although it is logical to think of these four qualities as occurring in order, this is not completely the case. The realization of the Vajrayana, where attachment to both the individual self and the self of phenomena has been fully eradicated, also penetrates the first three qualities to some extent. For example, seeing all teachings as practical instructions to pacify the afflictive emotions only truly occurs when self-attachment has begun to loosen. When self-attachment is strong and powerful, even if we wish to see all teachings as practical instructions, our preferences and biases will simply be too strong to genuinely view them in this way. We can understand the fourth quality to both follow the first three and permeate them to a greater and greater extent the longer the master trains and practices.

I would note here that nowhere in the explanation of rime is the assertion that all teachings are "one," as is sometimes expressed in the English language. It is quite a different thing to say that the meaning of the teachings is not contradictory and that they are mutually supportive than to say that they are one and the same thing. The Vajrayana is filled with many different methods that purify the mind, accumulate merit, and lead to realization. These distinct approaches are part of the special feature of the Vajrayana—while the vehicles below it rely upon only a few methods that everyone practices, the Vajrayana has many methods that can appeal to the different karma and dispositions of practitioners.

The rime approach does not do away with the distinct styles of teaching and methods that are presented by different lineages and schools of the Vajrayana. Rather, it does away with the emotional responses and judgments we often make toward them—for example, thinking one is better than another, or the willingness to apply one and not another. It would be more correct to say that due to the strong karma a practitioner has with a certain lineage, they practice that lineage as their main practice. Also, due to the practitioner naturally seeing the teachings of other schools and lineages as uncontradictory, they rely on those teachings for mutual support.

Lessons from Two Otherworldly Masters

In this modern era, it is rare to meet a genuine master who has renounced worldly life and dedicated him- or herself solely to the dharma in the style of a great vagabond such as Patrul Rinpoche, but I count myself among the fortunate. I was lucky enough to receive teachings on *Parting from the Four Attachments* from two such Longchen Nyingthig masters. The first was my own root lama, Tsara Dharmakirti Rinpoche, who taught at a large shedra in Kham, Tibet, presiding over several hundred monks and lamas. The second was Gyalgo Lama Tsepel, a nomadic lay yogi and an extremely close dharma friend of my lama.

On the outside, these two masters may have looked different. But they had strikingly similar ways of thinking, and the way they lived their lives shows just how closely they emulated the great lineage masters of old. My own root lama was an extremely disciplined *gelong* monk* who lived in a retreat room, which in Tibet we say is "just large enough for the four activities" of eating,

---

* A monk with full ordination.

studying, sitting, and sleeping. It had a shrine, a simple window to see outside, and a meditation seat that also became a bed.

Every day he woke us up at 3:00 a.m. to set up the shrine for morning practice. I remember in my late teenage years, several of his attendants and I would sleep on the floor next to his bed, dreading how quickly 3:00 a.m. would come. But day after day my lama was impervious to fatigue. After getting up at 3:00 a.m. to practice, he tirelessly followed a long daily schedule, alternating between teaching on different distinguished texts to the various classes of students at the shedra and completing his own daily *yidam** practices. If you have ever spent time with such a master, you will know what I mean when I say that his sheer ability to keep this kind of schedule was a sign of his realization, since it seemed beyond what was humanly possible. Tsara Dharmakirti Rinpoche was a distinguished scholar from Dzogchen and held the lineage of the Longchen Nyingthig that came directly from Patrul Rinpoche. His presence was authentic, magnificent, and incredible to behold.

Lama Tsepel, on the other hand, was a Khampa† in every sense of the word. He was a nomadic practitioner who didn't even start studying the dharma until he was thirty-seven years old. Due to his deep renunciation and devotion, he received pointing-out instructions on Atiyoga Dzogchen from the renowned Longchen Nyingthig master the first Alak Zenkar Rinpoche, who wore the white robes of a *tantrika*.‡ The first Alak Zenkar Rinpoche and his present living reincarnation, as well as Do Khyentse Yeshe Dorje in the nineteenth century, are recognized as reincarnations of Jigme Lingpa.

---

* Literally, a practice "bound to the mind," such that it is practiced continually by the practitioner.

† Lama Tsepel was from Kham, Tibet. Khampas have a reputation for being strong warriors who are direct and not overly concerned with etiquette.

‡ A lay practitioner of the tantras.

In comparison to my root lama, Lama Tsepel's study of the dharma was very brief. Where my lama had spent over twenty years at Shri Singha Shedra and his retreat room was filled with volumes upon volumes of philosophical texts, Lama Tsepel had only received the teachings contained on a few pieces of paper. These pages weren't wrapped in beautiful red silk like texts at my lama's shedra. They were covered in dirt from the cave where Lama Tsepel lived.

Lama Tsepel was dirty from head to foot. He looked as though he hadn't bathed for a long time. He had long, thick fingernails that he didn't cut, and he lived in a tiny dug-out cave in Gyalgo, an area of Tibet. It wasn't a natural cave but rather a hole in the mountain that had been used to mine gold. His room was cramped, just large enough for him to sit in meditation or sleep. It had a tiny makeshift shrine and a musty, unclean smell that made it unpleasant to enter. Once inside, it was difficult to sit comfortably and relax. You may not ever have met this kind of yogi before. He was a true *chattral*, a possessionless yogi, who had entered into lifelong retreat directly after receiving teachings from Alak Zenkar Rinpoche. Often in Tibet, this kind of retreatant is named after the place where they remain in retreat because they become a fixture of the place, just like the rocks, trees, and water. He was called Gyalgo Lama Tsepel because he never once left Gyalgo after he entered his lifelong retreat.

You may be wondering how two such masters, who were educated so differently and lived so differently, became close dharma friends. My lama said it was due to their deep realization of the Longchen Nyingthig lineage that they held such great respect and affection for each other. They also shared an affinity for the rime approach. For both, their wisdom was an expression of having deeply realized the nature of Atiyoga Dzogchen and thoroughly internalized, embodied, and utterly manifested the meaning of Sakya Drakpa Gyaltsen's masterful teaching.

How Sakya Drakpa Gyaltsen "Composed"
Parting from the Four Attachments

Even though we say that *Parting from the Four Attachments* was composed by Sakya Drakpa Gyaltsen, this isn't completely true. The words of this verse were spoken to him directly by Manjushri, who appeared to him as a body of light. After Sakya Drakpa Gyaltsen saw the face of Manjushri, he wrote a commentary on Manjushri's words and later became known as the author of the teaching. This is similar to how Shantideva received the entirety of *Way of the Bodhisattva* directly from the mouth of Manjushri, then gave teachings on transmission he had received while at Nalanda University, and is now credited as being the author of the text.

At the time Sakya Drakpa Gyaltsen received this teaching, his name was Kunga Nyingpo. In the dharma, it is common to receive new names when receiving important teachings or when taking different levels of ordination. This is how one person can come to be known by more than one name. The history of this teaching says that when he was just twelve years old, Kunga Nyingpo accomplished the practice of Manjushri—he directly saw the face of this deity and received its instructions. This may seem amazing for such a young boy, but Kunga Nyingpo had forged a connection with Manjushri in past lifetimes. According to the Vajrayana way of seeing things, the practice of Manjushri wasn't new to him, and it isn't incredulous that he could accomplish the practice of Manjushri as a young boy.

When he was twelve years old, Kunga Nyingpo stayed in a strict retreat, and after six months he accomplished the practice of Manjushri. First, he saw Manjushri directly, then he received this verse directly from Manjushri's own mouth. The four lines of this verse are incredibly profound because they are Manjushri's own words. They sound very simple, but because it is an upadesha-style teaching, its easy-to-understand words and meaning can be expanded to include the full essence of the sutra and tantra, as well as the complete wisdom of the lojong tradition.

Introducing the Lojong Tradition

The easiest way to understand the lojong tradition is to recall the lineages of masters who practiced and taught it. There are two main lineages of lojong teachings. One originates in the eminent master Jowo Je Atisha, whose main student, Drondompa, was the founder of the Kadam tradition of old. From there, the lineage was passed on to other renowned Kadampa masters, such as Chekawa Yeshe Dorje, who composed the seminal text *Seven-Point Mind Training*, which became the basis for mind training in the Kadam lineage.

The second lineage comes from Shantideva, whose most well-known work is *Way of the Bodhisattva*. The main form of mind training in this lineage is seeing others as equal to yourself, exchanging yourself for others, and making others more important than yourself. Gyalse Thogme Zangpo's essential text *Thirty-Seven Practices of a Bodhisattva* is also a part of Shantideva's lojong lineage. One of the unique and special qualities of Sakya Drakpa Gyaltsen's *Parting from the Four Attachments* is that it contains the meaning and wisdom of both of these lineages.

The modern Longchen Nyingthig lineage has a special connection with Shantideva's lojong lineage because Patrul Rinpoche is said to be a reincarnation of Shantideva himself. Patrul Rinpoche, who was also known as a great rime master, practiced, realized, taught, and composed many teachings on how to train the mind, following in the footsteps of Shantideva. He revitalized the study and practice of *Way of the Bodhisattva* throughout Tibet at a time when such teaching and practice were no longer in fashion; he taught on this text hundreds of times. Because my root lama trained at Shri Singha Shedra at Dzogchen Monastery, where Patrul Rinpoche turned the wheel of dharma for many years, he placed a major emphasis on both lineages of the lojong tradition, but especially on Shantideva's lineage as emulated by Patrul Rinpoche.

Taking the time to understand the way in which *Parting from the Four Attachments* contains the essence of all the lojong teachings is worthwhile. This verse is simple and easy to remember—we don't need to memorize volumes of texts and complicated philosophy to recall this one teaching—but that doesn't mean we don't need to contemplate its meaning in detail and make a personal application of its meaning. Jigme Lingpa said that if we don't raise our understanding of the dharma to the level of personal experience, our understanding "will fall off like a patch." This metaphor points out how even if we mend a hole on the elbow of our jacket, eventually that patch will wear out and fall off. It never becomes seamless and fully integrated. Likewise, if we leave our study of the dharma at the level of mere intellectual understanding, at some point we are going to separate from that knowledge because it hasn't become part of us.

How My Lama Embodied Sakya Drakpa Gyaltsen's Teaching

Tsara Dharmakirti Rinpoche was known throughout Tibet as a rime master who embodied the four great qualities articulated by Je Tsongkapa. However, since the remainder of the chapters that follow will discuss how Tsara Dharmakirti Rinpoche taught on the meaning of *Parting from the Four Attachments*, I will limit myself to explaining how his life, practice, and very presence embodied the meaning of this four-line verse. This will make his explanation of these teachings even more meaningful, as he was a master who practiced exactly what he taught.

If you are attached to this life, you are not a dharma practitioner. My lama embodied the meaning of this line by casting aside any attachment to what are called the eight worldly concerns: (1) hope for happiness and (2) fear of suffering; (3) hope for fame and (4) fear of insignificance; (5) hope for praise and (6) fear of blame;

and (7) hope for gain and (8) fear of loss. If we take a moment to reflect on these eight expressions of hope and fear, we may recognize that these hopes and fears consume a great amount of our time and emotional energy. This is true for most of us almost all the time. But my lama wasn't like this. He was wholly focused on the dharma and accomplishing the dharma for the benefit of sentient beings. He didn't have any personal demands for himself. He didn't care how others treated him, and he didn't wish to be the object of everyone's respect and reverence. Once, I was upset when I heard someone criticize him, and the advice he gave me was that I should never argue with someone else on his behalf or try to defend him. Instead, he told me just to follow his advice and show my good qualities as his student. Also, my lama was completely satisfied no matter where you put him. He embodied Patrul Rinpoche's famous advice to always take the lower seat.

The lojong teachings also say that the attachment we have to this life is shown by the strong habit of "preferring loved ones and disliking enemies." My lama didn't even harbor resentment toward those who tortured or harmed him while he was imprisoned in the 1960s. Later, when he encountered such people, we all witnessed how well he treated them, as though they were friends or honored guests. This is how he showed us the example of giving up all preferences for friends and dislike toward enemies, from the very root. His very presence was a wellspring of love and compassion that was so palpable that many students wept or couldn't speak or think in an ordinary way when they saw him.

As the meaning of this first line indicates, we cannot be a qualified dharma practitioner if we are tied up in worldly life. He was a fully ordained lama and kept all his precepts and *samaya** purely, free of damage. In Tibet we say that a qualified spiritual master

---

*   Samaya are commitments made by a student of the Vajrayana tradition that can never be transgressed.

"spits their worldly concerns like saliva in the dust, never to be taken back." If we think about the contemplative traditions, or even a profound tradition such as Atiyoga Dzogchen, we have to be available to practice and be present at every moment. Having given up the eight worldly concerns and preferences for loved ones over enemies, my lama was a true example of this type of spiritual master.

If you are attached to samsara, you do not have renunciation. The teachings say that renunciation toward samsara is viewing samsara like a nest of poisonous snakes, a mass of burning fire, or a land of cannibals. Once we see the nature of samsara in this way, we are exhausted by the very thought of living in this world and striving to find the happiness that ordinary beings seek, since we know deep down inside that such happiness is unattainable. My lama illustrated the meaning of this line by devoting his entire life to the dharma and not engaging in a single activity that was invested in trying to find the illusory happiness of samsara. His whole life was ceaselessly filled with the activities of the dharma and especially of a spiritual master: working at the view, meditation, and conduct; teaching, debating, and composing texts; examining the meaning of dharma texts and teachings; enacting the four types of enlightened activity; and accomplishing the practice of meditation.

If you have self-interest, you do not have bodhicitta. Although my lama was a realized master of Atiyoga Dzogchen, from the outer point of view he was constantly training in lojong and engaged in the activities of teaching and practicing the *Way of the Bodhisattva.* All his efforts and actions were focused solely to benefit others. He embodied the advice of the great Dzogchen masters of his lineage: "The view should be fearless; conduct should be cautious."

If grasping is present, it is not the view. In the presence of my lama, I didn't experience a single conceptual thought. Due to the power of his own realization, for short periods of time, those of us around him experienced what it was like to be free of grasping and to experience the unmistaken view of Atiyoga Dzogchen.

My Experience with Gyalgo Lama Tsepel

I've never been a person to go here and there seeking dharma teachings. But one day my lama told me that I should meet with Lama Tsepel, so I went. My meeting with Lama Tsepel constituted a very different kind of experience and instruction in the meaning of *Parting from the Four Attachments.*

As my lama wished, I traveled to the remote cave where Lama Tsepel lived; I was accompanied by Khenpo Tashi, an esteemed lama and elder from my shedra. At that time, I was studying at the shedra and paid a lot of attention to being clean and neat and living in a clean and neat environment. Meeting Lama Tsepel blew my mind.

When I entered the half-built temple below his cave, I was overwhelmed by the environment he lived in. It was exactly the opposite of the kind of place I lived in. Next, I noticed how dirty he was and how uncomfortable he must be in his matted sheepskin *gak* (winter robe) and bearskin hat. I looked around and saw that there wasn't anywhere to wash or bathe. Because of how he looked and my own attachment to cleanliness, I didn't have a strong feeling of devotion to him—the way one should when they are in the presence of a fully realized master—when I entered the room. I'm sure he sensed this. I knew I should do prostrations, so I tried, but he smacked me with his cane and told me to stop.

One strong memory I have of that experience was the evidence of his genuine contentment. Often the teachings tell us to cultivate an attitude of contentment so that we can reduce afflictive emotions such as dissatisfaction, unhappiness, jealousy, or envy. But Lama Tsepel was not cultivating contentment—he was actually content with everything. He was content with his clothing, his room, and even with the one pot he tossed literally anything into to make *thukpa* (soup). He had only one wooden bowl, which I'm sure he never washed. Instead, he licked the inside of the bowl after he was done eating and wiped it dry with his clothing. After we sat down, we had a meal together. He served me a bowl of the soup that he made. It smelled horrible, and I didn't want to eat it. In Tibet, it is not just rude but inauspicious to not eat what is served by a lama, so I forced myself to take a few bites. When I thought he wasn't looking, I poured it onto the dirt floor.

After we ate, we entered his cave, the old mine. I found myself not wanting to sit down on the floor because it was so dirty, but I did. What happened next was truly astounding. He said to me, "Khenchen Dharmakirti must have had a reason to send you to me. I heard that you are extremely smart and good at memorizing texts. If you applied everything that you have studied, you would already be a buddha." I felt that he could see right through me. His words shook me hard because I knew he was right.

Lama Tsepel had received very few dharma teachings. He had received instructions on *Parting from the Four Attachments* from Alak Zenkar Rinpoche, and in hindsight, his very appearance was the expression of the first line: "If you are attached to this life, you are not a dharma practitioner." He also received simple instructions on Dzogchen from Alak Zenkar Rinpoche, one or two pages that were composed by his previous incarnation, Do Khyentse Yeshe Dorje. He was content with what he had—and everything he had, he practiced and mastered completely.

Lama Tsepel went on to say, "The difficulty you have is that you haven't applied what you have learned, so you are still wandering in samsara. Your mind is completely separate from the dharma." His words made a tremendous impact. Often when I teach the dharma now, I reflect on Lama Tsepel's words—his advice seems to be the advice that is most needed in the modern world, to be heard and practiced by modern dharma practitioners. Thinking back, it is incredible that this lama, who seemed to have so little knowledge to impart, gave me some of the most profound teachings I have ever received.

Next, he opened his few *pecha* pages,* which I later learned contained *Parting from the Four Attachments* and a few pieces of advice he had received. The pages were old and worn, and dirty smudges had mostly covered up the words so they could no longer be read. He said to me, "I received pointing-out instructions and *Parting from the Four Attachments* from Alak Zenkar Rinpoche, and because I trained my mind and applied the meaning of these teachings completely, my lifespan and my accomplishment are equal." This is an expression we use in Tibet—it means that the practitioner's realization and accomplishment increases day by day, so the measure of life will equal the measure of realization.

Then he read through the four lines written by Sakya Drakpa Gyaltsen and gave his version of a teaching on it. First, he read, "If you are attached to this life, you are not a dharma practitioner." He didn't say much, but he said to me forcefully, "Do you know what that means? Have you understood it?" He didn't give any commentary on the words, he just said, "If you have attachment to this life, you'd better get rid of it! Understand?" My own lama's commentary on this verse, which will follow in the later chapters of this book, is so profound and eloquent. But I can't say that Lama Tsepel's commentary was any less powerful, though he expressed it in only a few words.

Next, he read, "If you are attached to samsara, you do not have renunciation." He didn't explain what renunciation is, the way a scholar would when giving the same teaching. He simply asked me in his gruff voice, "Do you have renunciation? You are a lama and an ordained monk. Without renunciation you aren't even

* A Tibetan-style book printed using woodblock carvings.

keeping your vows." Then he said, "I don't have any grasping or attachment to samsara." The difference between us was striking, and where I thought I looked like a dharma practitioner when I entered the cave, I realized now that he was the authentic yogi.

Then he said, "If you have self-interest, you do not have bodhicitta." He asked me, "Haven't you taken the bodhisattva vow? But isn't your only thought how to benefit yourself? If that's true, how can you train in bodhicitta and practice the bodhisattva path?"

Finally, he said, "If there is any grasping present, it is not the view." He asked Khenpo Tashi, "Tashi, what does that mean? Have you understood it? Have you understood it?" It was obvious from Lama Tsepel's presence, words, and conduct that he had thoroughly understood the meaning of this line and had completely realized the Atiyoga Dzogchen view.

When he completed this round of teaching, he reread the verse nine or ten times, and at the end he said, "Apply the dharma and make it inseparable with your own mind. No matter how long and hard you study, you will never find more profound instructions in the entirety of the teachings." And I could see myself for the first time—a young lama and scholar in training who was spending all my time receiving dharma teachings but not really applying the meaning of the dharma to myself.

This idea was expressed in Patrul Rinpoche's *Collection of Heart Advice* when he said, "If conduct is entangled with the world, there is no benefit." In other words, when we just study the dharma but don't apply it and use it to cut through our attachment to ourselves and the beings and world around us, our actions won't bear fruit. The efforts we make with body, speech, and mind won't be purposeful at all—our afflictive emotions won't decrease, and we won't experience any relief from suffering; our self-attachment won't decrease, and we won't experience any increase in our compassion and care for others. So even though it may look like we are fully devoting ourselves to spiritual practice, our efforts just reinforce the mental and emotional habits we already have and further entangle us with worldly life.

Also in this collection, Patrul Rinpoche said, "If contemplation is entangled with confusion, there is no benefit." If the mind doesn't follow the dharma but just remains confused and overpowered by ignorance, then what is the point of studying the dharma? Even if we understand the meaning of the dharma, if we don't apply it correctly and with discipline, but allow ourselves to remain confused—for example, because applying the actual meaning of the dharma is difficult—no change will occur. Our own mind is just going to remain the same as it is now, and our efforts at contemplation will bear no fruit.

When I returned to the shedra and arrived in front of my lama's tiny retreat house, he opened his window and asked excitedly, "Son, come here! How was it? What happened? What did Lama Tsepel say?" I recounted the whole story tearfully to my lama. He nodded with approval: "Very good, very good. The effort of sending you to see Lama Tsepel was worth it. In the future, don't forget this experience—a genuine practitioner of the dharma is just like Lama Tsepel." Lama Tsepel's words and teaching continue to impact me to this very day.

PART TWO

Commentary on *Parting from the Four Attachments*

In the tradition of Secret Mantra,* whenever dharma teachings are given, they are given in the style of "waves on the ocean." This means that the particular topic will be taught once, then again and again and again. This is done for several reasons. First, it supports most dharma students, who are unable to grasp the meaning of a teaching the first time around. Or even if we do, our understanding is limited. For example, we might think back to when we first started studying the dharma. What we knew then is probably much less than what we know now. Just so, our understanding of a particular teaching is colored by our experience and prior training, as well as our aptitude as a practitioner. Regardless, the first time we hear a teaching, it is likely to make an imprint and an impact. But that imprint and impact would be felt much more deeply if we were to hear that same teaching again, perhaps taught in a different way, from a different text, or articulated by the words of a different lineage master.

Another reason the teachings are given like waves on the ocean is that in the first wave, the teaching can be presented in a general way, to help students build a foundation. The next presentation

---

* The Vajrayana vehicle that includes teachings on Buddhist tantric practices.

can be more in depth and reveal more of the inner, more profound nature of the teaching. The next wave after that can expose even more of the direct meaning. This is why a teaching is often given from the point of view of the outer, inner, and secret—or as a commentary on the words and then an exposition of their meaning, as in this book. A teaching can also be given progressively, as many times as is necessary for students to fully understand the meaning. This is called giving "ripening instructions." The lama gradually guides the student to a deeper and more genuine understanding of the teachings so that the student begins to ripen and mature as a practitioner, becoming a more suitable vessel to receive increasingly more profound teachings. It is in this spirit, then, that we begin an exploration of the meaning of *Parting from the Four Attachments* and its natural complement, *The Four Dharmas of Gampopa.*

The First Line

If you are attached to this life, you are not a dharma practitioner.
If you are attached to samsara, you do not have renunciation.
If you are attached to self-interest, you do not have bodhicitta.
If any grasping is present, it is not the view.

A Language-Based Commentary on the First Attachment

The first line states, "If you are attached to this life, you are not a dharma practitioner." The commentary on the first line is the most crucial because it lays the foundation for all the teachings that follow. As practitioners of the dharma, we must know what it means to be "attached to this life" and what it means to cut through that attachment. Due to our upbringing and our culture's influence on our thinking, we may have a very different idea of what this means than is described in the traditional dharma. We might wonder, for example, if cutting through attachment to this life can be achieved through an attitude of simplicity, whereby we make little effort at earning money; don't spend a lot on clothing, shoes, or a car; and live in a home that has just the necessities. Many modern dharma practitioners view this type of material simplicity as cutting through attachment to this life. As a lifelong retreatant, Lama Tsepel certainly embraced this philosophy of simplicity.

However, although it shares some commonality with the idea of simplicity, the kind of genuine contentment that Lama Tsepel had was extraordinary. This contentment went far beyond adopting a lifestyle that wasn't focused on worldly success. His conduct showed something more than an affinity for simplicity. It showed that he didn't have a single care for himself, that he had given up attachment to this life completely. For example, he never once left the cave where he lived in Gyalgo, even to see a doctor if he was sick. He disregarded hardships such as cold, discomfort, hunger, and illness as attachments to this life that would distract him from dharma practice.

Lama Tsepel's example shows us that cutting through attachment to this life can't be achieved at the level of outer conduct alone. Even though we may adopt a lifestyle of simplicity on the outside, it comes down to what we have understood and realized in our own minds. Just because we look simple and unrestrained on the outside, have we reduced our attachment to this life at the level of the mind so that we express fewer and fewer afflictive emotions? Have we reduced our attachment to ideas, philosophies, politics, and so on, such that the number of conceptual thoughts, judgments, and criticisms that rush through the mind at every moment has begun to lessen? Because Lama Tsepel was fully convinced there was no benefit to working at any aspect of "this life," he gave up worldly life completely and became a possessionless recluse, content to live in a dug-out cave alone and practice the dharma. By casting aside all cares for himself and focusing solely on his spiritual practice, he destroyed his attachment to "this life" from the very root—to a degree that might be difficult to imagine.

Since our ordinary mindset does not enable us to live as Lama Tsepel did, we can conclude that cutting through attachment to this life must happen at the level of the mind. How can we do this? The Vajrayana tradition articulates a great number of methods and styles of practice to cut through attachment, but as the teachings say, "Of the body, speech, and mind, the mind is king." So, when we examine our attachment to worldly life and the way it obstructs us from practicing the dharma in a genuine way, we must start at the level of the mind.

What It Means to Be a Genuine Dharma Practitioner

The second part of this line points out that there is something called a "dharma practitioner." Since the Tibetan language relies on context and implication to convey full meaning, we can deduce that at the same time that Sakya Drakpa Gyaltsen points out that there is such a thing as a genuine practitioner of the dharma, he also implicitly points out that there are many charlatans, practitioners who are merely acting like they practice the dharma but are falling short for one reason or another. One type of practitioner may be ingenuous because they receive teachings based on the desire to use the dharma for material gain, status, wealth, or admiration. Another type of practitioner may have received the correct instructions for how to practice the dharma, but due to having too many attachments to this life, is too caught up in ordinary life's many tasks and pursuits to practice in a genuine way. And yet a third type of practitioner may not have been able to receive the proper teachings from a qualified lama, so although they may wish to do so, they are unable to put the dharma into practice authentically.

If these types of practitioners do not rise to the level of a genuine practitioner, then what is a genuine practitioner of the dharma?

We can get more insight into this question by examining the original Tibetan word for "dharma practitioner": *chospa*. This word has two syllables: *chos* and *pa*. In the Tibetan language, this word is formed by adding *pa*, a nominalizer, to the end of the Tibetan word *chos*, meaning "dharma." That addition of *pa* transforms the word "dharma" into a person—it becomes a "person who embodies the dharma" or who is the dharma itself. So, we could say that a dharma practitioner has made themselves one with the dharma.

Although we can generally understand that a dharma practitioner has brought the dharma into their heart and mind, there is no one description of what a genuine dharma practitioner looks like. If you think back to the two stories about my own lama and Lama Tsepel, they looked very different on the outside. But they were both genuine practitioners on the inside.

One way we can think about it is to say that for anyone who practices the dharma seriously, what it means to be a genuine dharma practitioner changes all the time. This is because we begin just where we are when we step onto the path—and this is individual and different for everyone. We have our basic understanding of what the dharma is at that moment. Then, as time goes on, we hear more teachings, receive more guidance, and apply the instructions we have been given, and we begin to transform. As a result, what we were doing before isn't genuine anymore—we must reembody the dharma each day with our new understanding to truly qualify as a dharma practitioner.

One of the things that happens to practitioners is that we can become complacent with our progress on the path. If we make a lot of effort that results in positive change and spiritual growth, we may be too easily satisfied. Once the intensity of our suffering lessens due to our own efforts at practice, we may forget that our attachment to this life is going to rear its head again and create more obstacles and misery for us in the future. This is the same old amnesia that all humans have about the suffering of this life.

It is difficult to remember that change and progress on the path needs to be gradual and consistent so that we don't fall into a state of laziness or procrastination.

Put another way, as our capacity to embody the dharma increases due to consistent application of practice, if we remain satisfied with what we were doing before, then we have fallen into the state of just pretending. This is because we aren't really focused on cutting through our self-attachment; we are just hiding out and trying to take a break from the suffering of ordinary life.

It can be extremely helpful to reflect on the benefits of consistent, disciplined effort. If we get into the daily habit of maintaining the efforts we make at dharma practice, then even during those times when we feel we have gained some ground, we will be able to rely upon that discipline to help us not fall into complacency and to continue practicing. We should also be mindful of our capacity and energy level. We don't want to wear ourselves out through inconsistent effort, sometimes working very hard and then dropping the ball. Instead, we should try to apply the same amount of energy, as though we are running a marathon rather than a sprint. As a genuine practitioner of the dharma, we shouldn't have the attitude, "I'm going to achieve something this year and then I can take a break." We should approach the dharma as a lifelong practice. We want to gradually move forward and take care not to backslide.

The Cares of This Life

One piece of profound advice on this topic was given by Jowo Je Atisha, who said, "Send this life's cares from the mind." This is such an eloquent way to direct us to stop investing our energy into this life. The eight worldly concerns mentioned earlier are examples of some of the "cares" of ordinary life. Another way of expressing this is trying to get what we want for ourselves—that is, getting wrapped up in our own wish for happiness. But for each person, the things that we care about most and are most attached to will likely be different.

Sometimes students ask me, "If I become a dharma practitioner, do I have to get divorced/stop doing things with my kids/quit my job . . ." and so on. Or "If I stop caring about ordinary life, won't I become cold and distant from everything and everyone I love?" Although we could certainly read Atisha's words to mean this, according to the teachings he gave, it isn't quite right. Again, we aren't dealing with our outer conduct as the measure of a genuine dharma practice. We are dealing with the level of the mind.

Our own suffering, which also causes and contributes to the suffering of others, is dependent on the degree of our self-attachment and the attachment we have to others and outside circumstances. For example, if we have strong feelings of attachment to loved ones, such as our spouse or children, we may have more expectations for them and put pressure on the relationship as a result. We may feel clingy or needy for their attention, or get emotionally upset if they don't treat us the way we want. All of these "cares" result from attachment rather than an unselfish feeling of love toward them. These "cares" are attachments and cause us much unhappiness and suffering.

On the other hand, if we cultivate more compassion toward our loved ones and focus on their happiness instead of worrying so much about ourselves, then these worldly relationships can help us be better dharma practitioners and more loving human beings. The issue isn't necessarily the way we arrange our lives but rather how attached we are to ourselves and others.

Dharma versus Ordinary Conduct

Patrul Rinpoche offered another way to think about the meaning of this first line. In *The Words of My Perfect Teacher*, he said, "Even though I have entered the path of dharma, I stray into ordinary conduct." This sentiment is perfectly on point. It describes the situation where we have the intention to practice the dharma but we are distracted by attachment to this life. In the beginning, we may think of the word *distraction* in a very general way. For example, we may be distracted by daily tasks and responsibilities to our family and employer. We may have developed habits that are distracting, such as looking at our cell phone often, ruminating over certain ideas or memories and getting lost in the past, or chasing after pleasurable experiences like eating out, shopping, or doing something relaxing and enjoyable with a loved one. All of these activities undoubtedly distract us from dharma practice.

If we had to make a list and prioritize the things most important to us, often dharma is low on the list—or even last. If we get busy, sick, or wrapped up in something—either happy or sad—dharma practice is often the first thing that we skip. If we can't make time for formal practice, we are unlikely to remember the dharma in ordinary life. When we are wrapped up in the distractions and attachments of ordinary life, we are likely not to remember to apply the dharma at all. All these situations illustrate the meaning of "straying into ordinary conduct" and how attachment to this life makes our dharma practice disingenuous and uncommitted.

Distractions also manifest on a much subtler level, including those from the five desirable objects of the senses. Our minds are filled with near-constant sensory input and reactions to what we see, hear, smell, taste, and touch. Thoughts and emotions then arise in response to this sensory input. There are also inner distractions, such as the arising of mind and mental factors,* and the eight types of consciousness.† Our habitual mind and the man-

---

* The mind and its mental factors are what apprehend objects in general and their qualities.

† The eight types of consciousness are the consciousnesses of sight, smell, sound, taste, touch, mind, the afflicted consciousness, and the alaya consciousness.

ifestation of karma that we have accumulated in the past serve as distractions even when there is no sensory stimuli. A simple recollection of a situation that makes us happy or sad can be enough to distract us and cause us to be literally lost in thought or emotion for hours, days, or even weeks. No wonder we feel too busy to practice the dharma! On a moment-to-moment basis, we are almost never present.

Ordinary conduct also manifests in the way that our behavior contradicts our formal study and practice of the dharma. For example, after we enter the Buddhist path, we take the bodhisattva vow, listen to teachings on *Way of the Bodhisattva*, and even train in bodhisattva conduct. But because of our prior habits and the strong attachment that we have to these inner and outer distractions, our conduct remains completely ordinary. For example, if we tend to want others to like us and speak well of us, we may continue to focus on ourselves and how to get what we want rather than focusing on how to apply the dharma. Even if we think we are applying the dharma when we are in fact entertaining a strong wish for admiration and praise, we have lost our intention to practice. Not only is our conduct still ordinary—we are reinforcing the very habits that we want to undo. In *Way of the Bodhisattva*, Shantideva said,

> Praise and compliments distract me,
> Sapping my revulsion with samsara.
> I start to envy others their good qualities
> And thus all excellence is ruined.*

If we are not really applying the antidote given in the teachings—in this case, to recognize our strong attachment to being

---

* Shantideva, *The Way of the Bodhisattva*, trans. Padmakara Translation Group (Boston: Shambhala, 2008), 152.

liked and spoken well of by others and reflecting on the meaning of Shantideva's words—we may think we are making effort at the dharma, but our dharma practice is never going to be strong enough to overcome the ordinary habits that we have. Those habits arise without any kind of effort on our part; on the other hand, applying the dharma requires great effort.

When we hear a sound or words that we don't like, it can feel like that sound is attacking us. This is how strongly we identify with our sensory experiences, one of our deepest forms of attachment. But we may never have thought of this strong identification as a distraction. It is not only a distraction but a distraction that consumes our time and energy and separates us from the dharma. This can really illustrate why reducing these kinds of distractions will benefit not just our peace of mind but also our ability to practice the dharma.

If we try to keep our lives just as they are and then add dharma practice on the side, we are never going to become a genuine practitioner of the dharma. Our attachment to this life brings us suffering and draws us away from spiritual practice. It doesn't make sense that we could leave the way we live our lives unchanged—full of attachments and distractions—and still transform spiritually.

Patrul Rinpoche also teaches that if the three doors—body, speech, and mind—remain ordinary, we won't gain a correct understanding of how to practice the genuine dharma. What does it mean for the three doors to remain ordinary? If we do not reduce our self-attachment by applying the lojong teachings, our mind will remain just as it is now. If the mind doesn't transform, then likewise no real and lasting change can come to our body and speech. In that case, because we have remained utterly the same, with the same worldly attachments and overwhelming self-attachment, we won't gain any insight into how to genuinely practice the dharma. We will simply view the dharma through the lens of our own self-attachment, as we have always done.

If we look around at modern practitioners of the dharma and examine ourselves, we can see that a great many people claim to practice the dharma but act just like ordinary beings. My lama used to say that when we have been introduced to the dharma and still behave selfishly, overwhelmed by our own desires and attachments, that we are worse than ordinary beings because dharma practitioners should practice what they study. They should not go here and there behaving unmindfully and acting unkindly to others. Patrul Rinpoche called people who act like dharma practitioners "dharma charlatans." They talk about the dharma and may even pretend to teach the dharma. They change the way they dress, the way they talk, and even carry a mala or prayer wheel. But they do all of this without making any fundamental change to the mind. The point of practicing the dharma isn't how we appear on the outside. Dharma should transform the mind. As Lama Tsepel told me, if we separate our mind from the dharma, there will be no benefit.

In all honesty, it's very difficult to make ourselves as one with the dharma because of the enormous amount of attachment we have to ourselves and this life. When we try to embody the dharma and practice it in a genuine way, we are faced with many choices. It is as though we are constantly facing a choice between "who we have been" and following the path of dharma. To follow the path of dharma, we have to give up a lot of our ideas and negative habits. So, in many ways, we must give up "who we have been" and "who we think we are"—that is, our own identities. This is because "who we have been" and "who we think we are" are laden with attachment. They are full of belief systems and self-fulfilling prophecies that won't allow us to apply the dharma as it is meant to be practiced.

It can be very scary for practitioners to realize that to practice the genuine dharma, one must gradually give up the identity that took a lifetime to build. However, if we think about it, it makes sense. Our identity makes us unhappy because it is an expression of self-attachment. The stronger we feel about "who we are," the more we are bound to suffer. We simply care more about how others see us, what we think we need, what others say, if we are being treated well enough, and so on. The more we care about our status and needs, the more dissatisfied and unhappy we feel. This is simply human nature. However, if we can relax a bit or turn that focus away from ourselves and simply think of others, we can finally take a breath of fresh air.

Gampopa's First Dharma

Grant your blessing so that my mind may turn toward the dharma.
Grant your blessing so that dharma may progress along the path.
Grant your blessing so that the path may clarify confusion.
Grant your blessing so that confusion may dawn as wisdom.

Having reflected on how the attachments of this life make it difficult for us to genuinely practice the dharma, let's turn to the first line of Gampopa's famous four-line verse to see how it can elucidate the meaning of Sakya Drakpa Gyaltsen's first line of *Parting from the Four Attachments*. Gampopa's first dharma states, "Grant your blessing so that my mind may turn toward the dharma." I find profound meaning in this line, which directs us to resolve the contractions and tension that we feel between this life and dharma practice.

We are so used to making this life important that we may not even feel there is a tension between our life and our practice unless we are trying to bring the dharma into our daily lives, activities, relationships, and so on. But once we begin to do that, we notice that the attachments we have to this life restrict our spiritual progress and make it difficult for us to apply ourselves to practice. This might happen due to our attachment to pleasure—perhaps we want to relax and enjoy ourselves rather than practice. It also might happen because training in bodhicitta is difficult; and to continually apply the lojong teachings, we must take responsibility for ourselves mentally, emotionally, and physically. Or it might happen due to the attachment we have to a particular relationship, which feels strained when we put too much time and energy into dharma practice rather than the relationship. Of course, there are a great many other cases where we feel tension and conflict between this life and the dharma, but the point is, for the mind to follow after the dharma, we must face and resolve all of these difficulties.

Even ordinary Tibetans faced this same situation when the dharma first arrived in Tibet in the eighth century. No one really knew how to follow the dharma at that time, so when Jowo Je Atisha first arrived in Tibet several hundred years later, many scholars and monks asked him to explain how to genuinely practice the dharma. Atisha's answer: "Don't make yourself so busy and so distracted. Don't let yourself be too attached to this life."

What did these words mean to Tibetans at that time? Maybe they thought letting go of worldly life meant abandoning their nomadic lifestyle. That may be true, but the most important thing that Atisha taught the Tibetan people was to cultivate positive actions, positive speech, and positive thoughts by focusing more on the dharma. If we compare the lifestyle in Tibet at that time to life in the modern world, it was much less busy and had many fewer distractions than we have now. If worldly life was already slow, then Jowo Je Atisha must have been referring to our inner life. In Tibet we still say, "Don't do too much . . . don't do too much."

We are all so busy—externally, internally, mentally, and emotionally—so when we apply the dharma in modern society, we need much more mindfulness and discipline. We need to make much more effort. This recalls one of Jigme Lingpa's teachings. He said that sometimes practicing and doing retreat is better than never doing it at all, but it's much more important to consistently apply the dharma. This teaching is especially good for modern practitioners to remember.

Gampopa's whole quotation is written in the form of a prayer. When you read it, you request the blessing of the lineage masters and beings who have realized the nature of wisdom so you can follow in their footsteps. Making aspirational prayers like these is necessary at the beginning, middle, and end of the path. We may think the mind follows the dharma, as when we first enter the path. But we are faced with situations every day where we can choose to apply the dharma or not, and we can choose to make the attachments of this life more or less important. Making this kind of prayer and supplication, no matter how long we have been practicing, is extremely beneficial. Additionally, Gampopa was a realized master of the Kagyu tradition. Despite the fact that he was a realized master, he still supplicated wisdom beings and lineage masters to bless him and to ensure that his mind didn't stray from the dharma. If this supplication benefits a master like him, we can be sure that it can also help us to enter the path of dharma correctly.

I also recommend making other kinds of aspiration prayers daily to ensure that our minds follow the dharma, not just now but for the rest of this life and then from lifetime to lifetime. We could make a prayer like this: "In all of my future lifetimes, may I meet with the perfectly pure dharma again and again. May I take a perfectly pure human rebirth again and again. May I meet with a perfectly pure lama in all of those lifetimes again and again. Not just me, but may all sentient beings have these same favorable conditions to practice the dharma and attain liberation."

In the beginning, our prayer may feel feeble or contrived. But if we pray continually in this way day by day, slowly it will gain strength. If we make this wishing prayer over a long period of time, eventually we will feel the power and strength of the prayer when we make it.

A Meaning-Based Commentary on the First Attachment

The concise meaning of the first line is that if we can't give up attachment to this life, the mind won't follow the dharma. What does it mean that the mind won't follow the dharma? It means that we can practice the dharma, but that dharma we practice is not pure. And if we practice the dharma in an impure or erroneous way, the dharma can't be accomplished. How does attachment to this life hinder us? According to the Vajrayana teachings, our dharma practice has a special potential to benefit us when we are dying. This is because all the elements, as well as the conceptual mind itself, dissolve as we die. During our lifetime, we struggle to work with the conceptual mind—but as we die, it falls away naturally. This is indeed a very special opportunity to realize the meaning of the teachings that we have trained in for a lifetime.

We could even say that as Vajrayana Buddhists, the reason we practice the dharma is to be able to practice at that all-important moment of death, when it is the most possible to attain spiritual accomplishment. Many Vajrayana practitioners—and especially yogis and yoginis who trained in Atiyoga Dzogchen—attained complete liberation as they were dying. Even though we may not reach the same spiritual accomplishment as they did, it is still possible for us to practice as if we are facing the moment of death. Some of the most important practices to support our spiritual death are training in bodhicitta, working on the lojong teachings, training extensively in *phowa*,* and reciting aspiration prayers to take birth in Amitabha's or Padmasambhava's pure land.

Why does attachment to this life make it difficult for us to practice the dharma as we experience the stages of dying and the moment of death itself? Death is a unique experience in that it is the moment when we literally lose everything—our body, mind, loved ones, possessions, identity, and so on. As we approach

* Literally, "transference of consciousness," a practice done at the time of death.

death, we become more and more aware of this overwhelming loss we will face. On one hand, if we have reduced our self-attachment and attachment to this life, then as we die, that experience is less terrifying. In other words, the less we care about losing ourselves, the less fear we have. But if we have spent our whole life cultivating attachment to our corporeal body and the life we have, then the moment of death is going to be extremely frightening. When we are dying, the mind is already in a feeble and weakened state as the elements dissolve one by one. If we are overwhelmed by fear, it won't be possible to remember to practice the dharma or put any teachings into practice.

It is important to be able to practice the dharma when we are dying because whatever state of mind we have when we die is a karmic imprint that propels us forward into the bardo state and our next life. When we are dying, if we are able to generate bodhicitta—the aspiration to place all sentient beings in the state of enlightenment, free of suffering—we may not experience any fear in the bardo state at all because of the all-encompassing love and power of that state of mind. This fearless, loving state of mind would lead us to take rebirth as a loving and compassionate person, with all the favorable circumstances of a dharma practitioner. Or, as another example, if we are able to rest in the view of Atiyoga Dzogchen at the time of death, at the very moment when all of the physical elements have dissolved and the conceptual mind itself is dissolving, we may be able to attain liberation free of the bardo state—or some other high level of spiritual accomplishment that would become the basis for our practice in the next lifetime and beyond.

However, if we don't make consistent effort at our Vajrayana practice and gain some qualities of accomplishment during our lifetime, then when we are dying, even if we have had a connection to the dharma for many years, it will be of no benefit. We will be just as attached to the appearances of dying, the moment of death, and the dawning of the bardo as we were to the appearances of our own ordinary lives. I must be honest—practitioners who believe they can remain enmeshed in the attachments of this life and gain spiritual accomplishment in the manner of the lineage masters at the moment of death are simply fooling themselves. If you think like this, you would be wise to give it up. Thinking in this manner will hinder your efforts at dharma practice. While we are alive, it is extremely important to gradually reduce our attachment to all of the various appearances and experiences of this life. If we are able to cut through the attachment we have to this life, the mind will follow after the dharma, and our dharma practice will increase and accompany us when we face the moment of death. Therefore, as the root verse states, it is extremely important to give up the attachment we have to this life.

Sakya Drakpa Gyaltsen also said if we cannot destroy our attachment to this life, entering the doorway of the dharma is of no benefit. We may think we are practicing the dharma by taking refuge and bodhisattva vows, or even by practicing meditation on a daily basis, but this is not enough to make our dharma practice authentic. We need to rely upon positive conditions that help the mind to follow the dharma. These positive conditions can only gather if we destroy the negative conditions that cause more attachment to this life. We could describe these negative conditions as the eight worldly concerns. We could also collectively describe them as the attachment we have to loved ones and the hatred we have toward enemies, as is generally stated in the lojong teachings.

The Obstacle of Being Attached to Strong Emotions

The worst condition for our dharma practice is being overwhelmed by strong emotions and failing to apply the dharma. If we look inward, we may see that our mind is often occupied by strong emotions, ideas, and attachment to how life should be. Considering that, it is worth asking, "If I truly feel justified in my thoughts and feelings and think they are right, what reason is there to apply the dharma?" Let's say we face a situation where we are angry. If we feel that anger is justified, we are less likely to think that we need to apply the dharma to give it up. Instead, we are more likely to think, "Why should I change? I didn't do anything wrong. They should change! They are the ones at fault." Unfortunately, when it comes to the suffering of life, there is no way to relieve it by keeping score. The more we invest in our emotions, the more energy and power they have, and the more our self-attachment sparks and blazes. When we understand this, it is easy to see how we create and prolong our own suffering whenever we believe that our emotions are valid, true, and justified. In *Way of the Bodhisattva*, Shantideva said,

> Those tormented by the pain of anger,
> Never know tranquility of mind—
> Strangers they will be to every pleasure;
> They will neither sleep nor feel secure.*

As Shantideva clearly states, the emotion of anger itself is suffering. The more attached we are to that anger, the more we suffer. It is the same with all emotions. Attachments to our emotions, perceptions, ideas, and beliefs are some of the greatest forms of suffering that all of us experience in this life.

If we start to notice that we are convinced that our own thoughts and feelings are valid, true, and justified, we may want to explore this further in the style of the lojong teachings. For example, we might reflect, "If my thoughts and feelings are correct, why do

---

* Shantideva, *The Way of the Bodhisattva*, trans. Padmakara Translation Group (Boston: Shambhala, 2008), 128.

they cause me suffering?" We also might want to question, "If I focused less on what I think and feel, could I be happier?" or "How would I feel if I spent more time focusing on the well-being and happiness of others?"

These inquiries get at the very heart of the lojong teachings. The Buddha taught, and the great masters all realized, that the emotions that arise based on self-attachment and attachment to this life are the true cause of suffering. These experiences, which are self-centered in nature, are different from the impartial love and compassion we train in on the path of dharma. If we are convinced that our thoughts and feelings are justified, true, and correct, we will not be motivated to break these deep emotional habits. Rather, this way of thinking ensures that our strong emotions and habitual thought patterns remain untouched and untamed by the dharma.

Distractions as Attachment to This Life

In addition to the emotions and belief systems we identify with, we are also involved in many distracting activities in our lives. The truth is, most of us simply don't have the physical, mental, or emotional space for dharma practice. Seeing this and having more self-awareness can be a good thing, but are we going to be able to dig up the roots of all these attachments and change our situation all at once? And if we can't, should we throw in the towel and quit practicing altogether?

We Tibetans have a saying: "When you put a dog on the roof, the dog always looks down and never looks up." We shouldn't be like this dog and discourage ourselves by thinking, "I'm not good enough." It is so easy for us to give up on dharma when we think this way. Instead, we should be like a bird in a cage who looks upward and wants to fly. This is the best attitude for a dharma practitioner: to want to improve no matter how difficult the current conditions or the road ahead.

The Kadampa masters of old took the long view of dharma practice. They practiced the dharma constantly and diligently, taking on hardship and making effort each and every day. They prepared to die each night by turning over their bowls to show that they may not eat breakfast the next morning. Then, the next morning upon waking, they renewed their diligent efforts at cutting through attachment to this life when they awakened. In this way, they showed how to gradually apply the teachings so that other practitioners would learn to reduce their own attachments to this life.

Is Work a Distraction?

Some students wonder about the necessity of working. After all, none of us modern Western practitioners can wander in poverty, living off the support and generosity of the dharma community to survive. Nor can we live in a forest hermitage like Patrul Rinpoche and his heart son, Nyoshul Lungtok. Our lives are just the opposite. Many of us spend eight or more hours per day, five or more days per week, working. We might ask, "Isn't this the biggest distraction from the dharma?" The answer is that it doesn't have to be. It depends on how we see the job that we do and how we engage in the practices of lojong while we are at work. For example, if we see our job through the lens of dharma, we can try to apply the dharma practice while we work. For instance, we might work on developing spiritual qualities such as patience and diligence, having generous and loving attitudes and interactions toward coworkers, and dedicating the work we do for the benefit of all sentient beings. We can also work with the intent to financially support our dharma practice by donating some of the money we earn to support our dharma center and dharma community.

Outside of work, we may want to consider the benefits of untangling ourselves from some of the other things that take up a lot of our time and aren't supportive to dharma practice. These might include drinking alcohol, watching television, playing video games, spending too much time on social media, being too involved with our phones, and so on. If we can reduce some of these activities and distractions, we will probably find it easier to develop a routine of daily practice and study at our dharma center.

The advice given by the masters is that we should give up whatever big and small things we can. Giving up whatever activities we can, even if they seem small or insignificant, can be a helpful support for spiritual practice. Of course, if you can give up something that takes up a lot of your energy, that's even better. But generally speaking, however much you are able to give up your attachment to this life, that's the degree to which your mind will follow after the dharma. The fewer attachments and distractions we have, the fewer obstacles our dharma practice will have.

How Does Attachment Create Suffering?

No matter what situation we are in, we generate attachment in the beginning, middle, and end of it. For example, at the beginning of an activity or situation, we likely have some kind of expectation or hope for how it will turn out: "If it turns out this way, I'll be happy." We may think we can reverse this way of thinking through our mere awareness of it or the mere knowledge that we are setting ourselves up for failure if it doesn't go well, but mere intellectual knowledge doesn't release us from attachment. This must be done through mind training and the continual application of dharma practice. As we begin something, we may also have other thoughts about the unhappy things we've experienced in the past, such as, "In the past I wasn't successful at getting things to turn out the way that I wanted, but this time I have figured out just the right way." Thinking in these ways ties up our energy and distracts us.

In the middle of the situation, depending on how it is unfolding, we may feel we have gained something or lost something. If we feel we have gained something, then we become attached to maintaining and keeping that thing and fearful of losing it. If we feel we've lost something, then we may feel attached to what we wanted or deny how the situation has turned out. Either way, we suffer due to our failed expectations. In all these cases, our attachment ties up our energy and distracts us.

In the end, we experience loss. This is a certainty. Loss will always occur sooner or later because everything that comes together will eventually come apart. Take a relationship as an example. In the beginning, it can seem like the relationship is going well and is in line with our expectations. Then in the middle, all kinds of things can happen—the relationship doesn't turn out how we expected, we become dissatisfied with the partner we chose or the way they treat us, we decide we want something different, we require the other person to change, and so on. Finally, either the relationship itself ends or at some point one of the partners dies. No matter how well or how poorly we get along, sooner or later, separation comes. We have all faced the painful results of attachment many times. If we wish for our mind to follow the dharma and practice the dharma purely, we can look to the spiritual masters for inspiration and direction. In the spirit of Lama Tsepel, we can cultivate a greater sense of mental and emotional contentment with what we have and try to be satisfied with the situation at hand instead of wishing for something better. We can engage in actions to make a situation that we are facing healthier or more positive, but we can also do so with an attitude of contentment and serenity, with less emotional stress and agitation.

Facing Enemies

We may think our problems come from the outside and that our cyclic unhappiness is caused by some kind of real or metaphoric enemy. Whether or not we relate to the idea of having an actual outer enemy that makes things difficult for us, it sometimes seems that other people or situations get in the way of our happiness or obstruct us from getting what we want. We have all had moments where we felt like the world is against us. But according to Sakya Drakpa Gyaltsen's first line, it's our own attachment to ourselves and this life that creates the obstacles we are facing. Because of our attachment to this life, we cannot accept whatever situation is at hand, and we view the situation itself as a hindrance or problem. Our lack of acceptance causes physical, mental, and emotional stress and suffering. We become tied up in our dissatisfaction and cannot apply the dharma. We should examine this for ourselves. Have we been facing a similar kind of obstacle in our dharma practice? If so, we should take steps to change this self-defeating habit of thinking.

From the point of view of the lojong teachings, we work on ourselves on the inside because trying to deal with outer ene-mies is a fruitless endeavor. Even though the outside world may manifest in exactly the way we wish it would, because we have self-attachment, we will still find a way to be unhappy and dis-satisfied with even the most perfect of situations. How many times have we thought, "If I just had [fill in the blank], I would be happy." Then we get the thing we want, but our happiness is short-lived. That is why attachment is called one of the emotional poisons.* When we are poisoned by attachment, we are bound to suffer. When self-attachment is present, we never feel content.

Tsara Dharmakirti Rinpoche gave the advice that all weapons, whether they be arrows, swords, or any other kinds of weapons, should all be turned inward toward the enemy of self-attachment. We should never invest our energy in inflicting harm upon outer enemies. If we gradually apply this way of thinking to the attach-ment we have to all the various appearances of this life, slowly

---

* The five poisons, or root afflictive emotions, are anger, desire (or attach-ment), ignorance, jealousy, and pride.

but surely our attachment will gradually reduce and can even be reversed. Reversing self-attachment completely is called *attaining liberation from samsara*. Countless practitioners have achieved this on the path to enlightenment. Although it is difficult, there is nothing that cannot be done without correct application and perseverance.

Without reversing the afflictive emotions, there's no way to give up attachment to this life. Here's a metaphor to consider. If your house was on fire, what consequence would come if you put more wood on the fire? What would happen if you called the fire department to spray water on the fire? When we reinforce our emotional habits and follow our ordinary way of thinking without applying the dharma, it is like putting wood on the fire. When we apply the antidotes taught in the dharma to our emotional state, this is like spraying water on the fire. At any moment, the choice is ours. We can fan the flames of our emotions or try to cool them down and take them to the spiritual path. When we see things through the eyes of our afflictive emotions, we may feel justified in what we feel and think, "I should be angry. I should yell at this person; they deserve it." We may not realize we are burning down our own house! I encourage you all, don't toss more wood on the fire. Pick up the lojong teachings and work on taming your mind.

In a sense, the emotions are inseparable from the mind. Often we identify so much with our emotions that when we experience them, it's hard to tell that it is just a feeling because it feels like "it's me." Using the lojong teachings, we can learn to separate from our emotions a little bit, at least intellectually. We can say to ourselves, "I'm not going to identify with this feeling so strongly. This feeling isn't real and will pass." If we put some space between ourselves and our emotions, we may be able to start making some different decisions. When anger blazes up, it would be extremely helpful to realize we are angry and need to watch our behavior, our energy, and our speech. These seem like small efforts and small situations, but approaching them this way time after time is the way we reduce our attachment to this life.

The effort we make at lojong practice is similar to the way tea makers make the very best tea in China. In China I have heard stories that the very best tea is made from dewdrops collected from the leaves and flowers on the hillsides. A lot of patience is required as dew can only be collected one drop at a time. When we train in lojong, it is a bit like this. We must make an effort to collect each and every drop of patience and tolerance, but the result is exquisite and wonderful. It is important to recognize that our efforts to apply an antidote to the afflictive emotions will only be successful some of the time. But then if we project that forward, thinking, "My success today shows I will also be successful sometimes in the future," we can gain confidence that slowly those small efforts will add up over time. Over a long period of time, we can really begin to reverse the attachment we have to this life.

Some Concluding Words and Advice on the First Line

This first line of *Parting from the Four Attachments*, spoken directly by Manjushri, is the foundation for the whole path of the dharma. Without the willingness to let go of the attachments we have to this life, practicing the path of dharma in a genuine way is not possible. We are all capable of letting go of attachment to this life, but somehow we don't. We have many reasons, excuses, and justifications to leave ourselves, our habits, and our self-attachment just as they are.

This is the reason many Vajrayana practitioners in ancient India and Tibet left society and went to the wilderness. They wanted to completely commit themselves to the dharma. Living as part of society, a community, or a family is laden with attachment and always brings difficulties. Today, none of us are likely to leave society and live as a wandering yogi, but we are capable of training our mind. We are capable of reducing our self-attachment and the attachment we have to this life. If we do that, we will follow the path of dharma in a genuine and sincere way.

The Second Line

If you are attached to this life, you are not a dharma practitioner.
If you are attached to samsara, you do not have renunciation.
If you are attached to self-interest, you do not have bodhicitta.
If any grasping is present, it is not the view.

A Language-Based Commentary on the Second Attachment

Sakya Drakpa Gyaltsen's second line states, "If you are attached to samsara, you do not have renunciation." To begin to develop a deeper understanding of the unique meaning of this line, let's first examine the words included in the verse, beginning with "this life" and "samsara." What is the difference between these two phrases? The word *samsara* is almost synonymous with "this life." Both phrases refer to our experiences of everyday life, but the meaning of "this life" is limited to only our current lifetime's experiences, while the meaning of *samsara* is greater than this. Samsara is the sum of our habitual patterns and emotional tendencies that repeat not only during this life but from lifetime to lifetime.

The literal meaning of the word *samsara* is "to circle" or "to cycle." Often samsara is depicted as a wheel that is referred to as the wheel of existence. The wheel of existence depicts the three realms of ordinary existence, which extend from the tip of the higher realms to the bottom of the lower realms. Within the wheel are the six classes of beings—beings in the hells, pretas, animals, humans, asuras, and gods.

The existence of the six classes of beings living within the three realms of samsara is like a bunch of bees trapped in a jar. The bees fly up and down, up and down, circling around and around without interruption. The Buddhist teachings similarly describe all of us sentient beings circling in samsara from lifetime to lifetime. Like a bee, we can't get out and don't have anywhere else to go, so we just circle around the wheel of existence again and again because there is no escape.

When we circle in samsara from lifetime to lifetime, what is doing the circling? From beginningless time until now, it is our consciousness that has been circling around samsara without interruption. Our consciousness is being propelled by the habitual tendencies of the mind and the karma we have accrued in the past. Habitual tendencies and karma, in turn, accumulate based on strong emotions and repetitive thought patterns.

For example, if we are an angry person who often gets upset and impatient, and we do not try to reverse or purify that pattern, we will be propelled by the energy of that anger now and in the future. Our anger will gradually increase over the years as we age during this lifetime, and when we take rebirth again, our mind will have the habit and the deep karmic imprint of anger. In future lives, we will start out as an angry person, and throughout that lifetime again, our anger will gradually increase. This deep habit of anger not only affects our mood and our relationships—it also fundamentally affects the way we see the world. The deep habits and imprints on the conscious mind—the karma we have accumulated in this and our previous lives—are what cause the appearance of the three realms and six classes of beings that make up the wheel of existence—samsara itself. When we see through the lens of our own karma, habits, and strong afflictive emotions, this is called karmic perception.

For example, if we are a person who continually cultivates the habit of anger and is propelled forward by that karmic tendency from lifetime to lifetime, at one point a dark and violent place like a hell realm will appear as the expression of our own heavy karma. This karmic perception appears because our perception is colored by our experience based on whatever strong karma we have accumulated. The hell realm we perceive may not look exactly like what you read about in a traditional Buddhist text— but what appears to us would certainly be characterized by fear, violence, anger, and rage. Our mind would express that karmic appearance of a hell realm because of the emotion of anger we have been expressing for so long. It is the same for any strong emotional tendency. Thus, in the Buddhist teachings, we say that samsara is an expression or a "self-appearance" of our own mind. In other words, we view the world around us through our own karmic perception.

Karmic perception is a key idea that helps us understand how samsara works, and it also explains how realization gradually dawns. In the previous example, we saw how karmic perception relates to the overwhelming tendency to express a strong emotion such as anger, which then leads us to experience profound suffering. But what if we spend our lifetime accumulating merit and purifying our mind's dominant habitual tendencies through the lojong teachings? This would also transform our perception. In this case, however, we would begin to perceive the world with greater ease, generosity, friendship, kindness, and so on. This is the way pure perception begins to develop. Although we still accumulate karma and perceive through the eyes of karma, the mind's self-appearance and how we view the world becomes a supportive condition for dharma practice due to our merit and purification. This is the very beginning of the path to realization.

We often engage with our emotions in an unbridled way because we believe in them, just as we believe in our own perception. We don't think that our perception is karmic perception; we think it is objectively real. If it is real, we are not at fault for reacting to our five senses and treating all our mental and sensory experiences as true and objective information.

As a result of believing in our emotions, point of view, and beliefs, we don't see the faults of samsara. Instead, we get caught up in habits that the lojong teachings refer to as "caring for loved ones and disliking enemies." All of our love and hate (even our mere preferences and dislikes), as well as our hopes and fears, are forms of strong attachment that are bound to bring us suffering because it is impossible to get and keep what we want, and unwanted things are continually occurring.

Because we believe in our emotions, we do not examine the nature of samsara, and we have no way to determine that its very root is self-attachment. Instead, we focus on the innate habit of grasping at "I and mine." Because we focus on I and mine—the very definition of twofold self-attachment—we continually increase our karma and afflictive emotions. This propels us forward and we continue circling in samsara. This constant circling creates many difficulties for us. We cannot see the faults of samsara because we are invested in samsara. We want samsara to make us happy, but the nature of samsara is always bittersweet. Even in the moments we feel happy, suffering has already begun to seep in. For example, we may have wished for an intimate love relationship and finally found "the one." But due to the impermanent nature of life, that relationship is bound to go through changes—conflict, hardship, pain, and eventually separation. This is an example of one of the three types of suffering within samsara: *the suffering of change*.* Because of our deep attachment to samsara, we can't accept it when changes occur and the things we are attached to don't continue the way they used to be. But we persist in our beliefs. We stubbornly do not want to give up believing that samsara can make us happy.

We can't see the faults of samsara because of the deep attachment we have to our own perception. Not only do we not realize

---

* The three types of suffering are the suffering of change, the suffering of suffering, and the suffering of everything composite.

that our perception is influenced by karma but we also believe that samsara is pure. The teachings say, "We see what is impure as pure." Samsara is as impure as a toilet, but most of the time we think it is wonderful because of our karmic perception. We see suffering as happiness because we wish it was so, and we refuse to accept that things are not the way we wish they were.

Because suffering inevitably manifests in samsara, we are constantly disappointed by the life we have. Even though there is no lasting happiness to be found in samsara, we mistake what is bittersweet for happiness, willfully forgetting the nature of suffering for as long as we can. As Padmasambhava said, "There isn't even as much happiness in samsara as can be found on the tip of a needle." We suffer continually because we cannot get what we want and must endure what we don't want. Everything changes moment by moment. Even if we get what we think we want, we lose it sooner or later.

Based on the five afflictive emotions of ignorance, anger, desire, jealousy, and pride, we suffer emotionally and happiness evades us. It doesn't matter what Buddhist vehicle we practice—the Mahayana, the general Vajrayana, the outer tantras, the inner tantras, or the unsurpassable tantras of Atiyoga Dzogchen—if we don't use our practice to cut through our attachment to samsara and develop the mind of renunciation, we will not attain liberation from samsara.

What Is Renunciation?

Great masters such as Sakya Drakpa Gyaltsen, Tsongkapa, Gampopa, Longchenpa, Patrul Rinpoche, and others encouraged Vajrayana Buddhists to develop renunciation because it is an absolute necessity for genuine dharma practice. When we have renunciation, we are so disappointed by ordinary life that we are willing to work extremely hard at the dharma to transcend it. It is a wonderful state of mind that fuels our enthusiasm to practice the dharma. Like the first line of *Parting from the Four Attachments*, the meaning of the second line comes down to our ability to practice the dharma in a genuine way. Without the mind of renunciation, we do not have the courage and strength to practice the dharma so that we can attain liberation, freedom from samsara. In the *Aspiration to Generate Bodhicitta, Utterly Pure and Supreme*, Patrul Rinpoche said renunciation "is the gateway to the path of liberation."

In the Tibetan language, the word for renunciation—*ngesjung*—has two syllables. The first syllable, *nges*, means "certainty." Renunciation requires us to develop the certainty that ordinary life in samsara is full of suffering and to give up the hope that it can bring us happiness. So based on this first syllable, we know (at least intellectually) that all beings are suffering. As Milarepa taught, the rich have the rich's suffering, the poor have the poor's suffering. Each person has their own accordant suffering, and for beings living in samsara, there can be no lasting happiness—no joy that isn't already tinged with sorrow. Ordinary life is suffering because we are the creators of our mental and emotional suffering. Whatever emotional patterns we already have, we simply repeat them, and suffering results. Whenever we reinforce the patterns we have, more suffering results. This is the cycle of samsara at work.

The second syllable of the Tibetan word for renunciation, *jung*, means "to be born from" or "to escape." Renunciation is the mind that is born from the knowledge that the nature of samsara is suffering. Additionally, when we have this understanding of the suffering of samsara, we develop the conviction to leave it behind or transcend it.

Samsara is like a prison, but not any ordinary prison. It is like Alcatraz—isolated, impenetrable, and inhospitable. If we were wasting away in Alcatraz with a life sentence, and on top of that we also saw how much everyone else was suffering, it would be unbearable. In prison we do not have nice clothing to wear or proper food to eat. We live in a damp and cold environment. We are lonely and bored, and may even be beaten by guards or other inmates. And because we are trapped in Alcatraz in the middle of the ocean, escape is completely hopeless. There is no way to whitewash that environment and make it seem happy—day after day, it is miserable. We can be as certain of this as we can that the nature of samsara is suffering. The feeling we would have if we suddenly found a way to break out of that prison—that is the meaning of "to be born from" and "to escape." When we are certain no hope is left and see truly that samsara is suffering, we renounce the cycle and find our way onto the path of dharma.

The idea of being trapped or confined within samsara raises the idea of freedom. How do we free ourselves from this constant cycling and recycling of human emotions, patterns, suffering, and self-defeating behavior? Returning to our metaphor, as a bee circles around the jar, it seeks freedom and escape from what confines it. This is logical. Similarly, why wouldn't we want to find a way out of this wheel of life that is so full of difficulty, hardship, suffering, and fear? We all wish for freedom, but the way that ordinary people and dharma practitioners seek freedom is very different.

In the modern world, many people choose to express freedom through means of individual expression and speech. They dress how they want, eat what they want, say what they want, and try to break down or escape the confines of cultural rigidity, tradition, and expectations. Some people protest on the street for certain causes or advocate for individual rights as the way to express their freedom. It can even be said that in Western culture, the unimpaired right to express our individuality is one definition of freedom. This way of thinking is the essence of democracy and social justice.

Buddhists think differently. Although having the freedom to do what we like and be who we want opens up many possibilities, a

Buddhist asks this the fundamental question: "Can this type of freedom truly free me from the suffering of samsara?" According to the traditional Buddhist teachings, this would never be possible because all these types of so-called freedom are just bandages meant to temporarily distract us from what hurts. What hurts is the nature of samsara itself—with all its change, disappointment, and heartache. What hurts is never being able to get or keep what we want and experiencing devastating loss. We cannot outthink, outsmart, or outmaneuver the nature of samsara. One day, each one of us will lose everything no matter how carefully we try to construct our life to make it calm, sane, and meaningful right now. That is why Buddhism points us in the direction of cutting through our self-attachment. That way we can try to heal the wound itself rather than just cover it up so it doesn't fester.

Vajrayana Buddhists believe that time is beginningless, and from beginningless time until now, we have taken birth in samsara an inconceivable number of times. We believe we have been living out and hardening our emotions, habits, and ways of thinking over many, many lifetimes. When we reflect on what it is like to live in samsara, we may realize we don't like it. We may realize it is brimming with all kinds of pain, loss, disease, and fearful situations. However, our attachment binds us to samsara. We cling to it.

It is only through the mind of renunciation—a state that emerges from our certainty that the nature of samsara is suffering—that we can cut through attachment to the endless cycles. However, developing this state of mind is extremely challenging. Even if we do achieve it, we forget it so easily. On a bad day when we are struggling emotionally, we may feel that we are willing to do whatever it takes to follow the path of dharma to the very end. But just like a rubber band, we quickly snap back to the same old habit of placing all our hopes, expectations, and dreams on this life in samsara. This changeable attitude is never going to enable us to cut through our attachment to samsara.

Three Supportive Qualities Articulated by Longchenpa
Longchenpa clearly articulates the meaning of the second attachment in *Nine Articulations of "What's the Benefit?,"* which emphasizes renunciation as the first quality, the very basis of dharma practice:

> Without the recollection of renunciation, weariness, and
>   death
> Practicing the dharma to gain enlightenment is just
>   superficial. There is no benefit.

Another meaning of *renounce* is "to reject." What is being rejected in this case? We reject the normal way that people think about this life and samsara. Most people believe that happiness results from doing hard work and trying to get the things that we want, but dharma practitioners reject this way of thinking. We become disillusioned by all the suffering, loss, and injustice that colors life in samsara. Life simply isn't fair, and there is no way to make it be so. We can do our very best and things still turn out badly. We can work extremely hard to get what we want, only to realize the thing we got isn't what we wanted to begin with. We may begin to realize that sooner or later, all our efforts will result in suffering and loss. At the same time, we may begin to see that our unhappiness and dissatisfaction come from within and cannot be cured by all of the things we have been trying to use to make ourselves happy.

As for the second quality, weariness, this has to do with becoming tired of all the activities of ordinary life that cause suffering and provide no real benefit. We have so many responsibilities, and there is so much to do all the time. We may experience these activities as positive or negative, but they are all fleeting, like waves on the ocean. One thing occurs, and right after that another, and another, and another—it's endless. What do we gain from all this effort? Exhaustion, for one thing. Stronger afflictive emotions and habits, for another. It is completely unlike practicing the dharma, where we have the chance to build up our spiritual strength whenever we apply it.

When we think about life in this way, we can develop a tremendous kind of weariness toward the activities of ordinary life. No matter how much we accomplish, we will always have more to do. We will never be finished. What is the nature of these everyday activities and responsibilities? According to the dharma, they are things that bring short-term benefit and are of no long-term consequence. Why is this? Because we can't take any of them with us when we die. From this point of view, most of the things we spend our time on are meaningless. Dharma is the only thing that can benefit us at the moment of death and the only thing we can take with us into our future lives besides the karma that we have accumulated. Everything else we do is like drinking salt water. Whether it be making money, being with loved ones, having a good time, or relaxing, no matter how much we have, we still want more.

Longchenpa's words have an additional implied meaning if we read carefully. Renunciation and weariness with samsara is necessary to attain enlightenment—simply performing good actions or being a good person won't do it. If the ordinary virtues of body, speech, and mind could accomplish enlightenment and buddhahood without renunciation and weariness with the nature of samsara, the world would be full of yogis and siddhas. Good people are doing good actions all the time. But those people aren't accomplishing the realization of the great masters because their minds are not tethered to the dharma—they are bound to this life in samsara.

Think of the temporary happiness that we invest in every day. We invest in relaxing, good food, finding enjoyment and happiness. We invest a lot of our time in love and relationships and the fantasy of how we want these to play out. But when we examine the nature of these relationships, we see they are also just like waves in the ocean. The ups and downs of a relationship are end-less—as is the wish to fix the relationship, the other person, or ourselves. If we cultivate the mind that is weary of samsara, we can begin to find a way to engage in that relationship while still maintaining a focus on the dharma. Otherwise, that relationship will be just like any other mundane activity that keeps our mind separate from the dharma.

The third quality Longchenpa asks us to recall is the nature of death. As Jigme Lingpa said, "Life is setting like the afternoon sun and death is creeping closer like an evening shadow." If we don't reflect on the meaning of death now, if we put off contemplating the impermanent nature of life, it will be too late to practice the dharma. If we had one pair of shoes to wear during this lifetime, a practitioner of the genuine dharma would notice that the soles were wearing out day by day as we walk closer and closer toward death. Our awareness of death would be the companion of our spiritual practice.

But this isn't so for people who don't practice the dharma. If we suddenly were to realize that the soles of our shoes have worn out and death is imminent, it is already too late to practice the dharma. The real benefit of dharma practice comes when our awareness of the impermanent nature of life acts as the motivation and driving force behind a lifetime of genuine dharma practice rather than dawning in the mind when death is near.

As Longchenpa instructs, it is important that we try to increase our renunciation and weariness toward the activities and life in samsara if we wish to develop a solid dharma practice that we can rely on in the face of the suffering, especially at the moment of death. We should remember that death can come at any moment.

What happens if we don't train in the impermanence of this life? Even though we may look like a dharma practitioner on the outside—someone who holds a mala or prayer wheel, reads sadhanas, recites mantras, or engages in different kinds of practices—without this conviction in the impermanent nature of life, everything we do is simply ordinary worldly dharma. When we are not training in the impermanence of life, there is no antidote to self-attachment, and there is no way to cut through attachment to this life. Without an antidote that cuts through attachment, any practice we do is ordinary, and we do not take any steps on the path toward enlightenment.

If we want to practice in a genuine way, we need to deeply reflect on and internalize the impermanent nature of life. If we reflect on the nature of impermanence constantly, then even in the dream state we will remember impermanence since we are thinking about it all the time during our daily life. When we get to the level of remembering impermanence even in the dream state, it's possible to truly renounce samsara and cut through our own attachment.

To reverse our attachment to samsara, as we are instructed to do in the second attachment, we can come back to the three qualities included in Longchenpa's quotation: renunciation, weariness with samsara, and impermanence. These are the essential qualities that we need to take as our companions on the path of dharma. In Tibet, we say a person's vitality is supported by their heart, life force, and eyes. We know that we are alive because we have these three things. We can think of renunciation, weariness, and impermanence as our heart, life force, and eyes of our dharma practice.

Advice from Gampopa on Developing Renunciation

I will return to the commentary on Gampopa's *Four Dharmas* a bit later, but first I wanted to include a few other pieces of advice he offered related to renunciation. In *Gampopa's Oral Advice: Precious Garland of the Supreme Path*, Gampopa said, "Suffering is the cause for developing renunciation." These words express the idea that, as a dharma practitioner on the path of genuine dharma, suffering is not a bad thing because when we are suffering, we have many opportunities to apply the dharma.

We all experience so much suffering every day. Some of our suffering is physical suffering—we may be getting old and experiencing a decline in our physical health. We may get woken up at night by back pain, shoulder pain, or leg pain. We may also have a chronic health condition or a disease, which not only causes us physical discomfort and pain but also causes anxiety and fear in ourselves and our loved ones. In addition to physical suffering, we also face emotional suffering. Once an emotional pattern starts, we tend to get totally wrapped up in it such that it is hard to think of anything else. On top of this, we also experience mental suffering. It can be especially painful when we encounter situations that seem unjust and are hard to accept. For example, upon learning that a loved one is seriously ill, we might feel angry and unwilling to accept the news.

When we are unable to accept emotional or mental suffering, it can turn into physical suffering. For example, when we experience a great emotional shock, we may literally become sick. Likewise, when we suffer physically, we often get emotionally upset and mentally unstable. We might become frustrated, angry, or depressed by a certain situation, illness, or injury. This massive pile of suffering, where additional suffering heaps itself upon suffering we are already experiencing, is called "the suffering of suffering." Even when it seems like we are about to hit the breaking point with our suffering, suffering never stops piling up. This doesn't have to be discouraging. If we know how to use all of these myriad sufferings as a cause to connect with dharma, our suffering can have a wondrous quality. Every one of these sufferings can be the cause of renunciation.

If we are able to see suffering from the perspective of a dharma practitioner, we can lose some of our feelings of frustration or anguish toward this life. Often when we are suffering, all we want is to get rid of it as soon as possible. Gampopa's words can lessen how intensely we dislike the experience of suffering. After all, disliking the experience of suffering only intensifies the experience that is already making us miserable.

Gampopa also said, "Suffering is the cause for developing certainty. Therefore, we can see suffering as the spiritual guide." To be able to do this requires a lot of mental training. Here again, certainty refers to renunciation—certainty in the nature of samsara is the source of all dharma practice. Because suffering brings us to renunciation, which helps us follow the path of dharma, our suffering is as essential and paramount as our spiritual teacher.

Our renunciation must be extremely deep for us to be able to see the experience of suffering as a spiritual teacher. Many practitioners have shallow renunciation because they are tired of the life they are living and want to find something that will make them feel a little bit better. This kind of renunciation is like being in a bubble bath. All the bubbles on the surface of the water are fragile and short-lived. We need strong renunciation to stick with the path of genuine dharma, otherwise our spiritual endeavor will pop like a bubble, and we will lose our way and stray from the path.

As Buddhist practitioners, we need to realize that samsara is a miserable place to be. We each need to be able to say, "Although it is difficult, I cannot blame this on anyone. I cannot blame my suffering and unhappiness on my family, spouse, boss, friends, community, spiritual teacher, dharma brothers and sisters, and so on. Whatever suffering I'm experiencing is created by my own self-attachment." This is how we treat suffering as a spiritual teacher and use it to eradicate our own afflictive emotions through the application of lojong practice. To be able to eradicate this formidable cause, we need to put dharma first in everything we do.

Gampopa also said, "Happiness and joy are the root of samsara. Reduce attachment to happiness and joy because they are demons that make obstacles to accomplishing the dharma." Happiness is the root of samsara because we want it so much, and we are so attached to it. Many times in the lojong teachings we are told to take suffering to the path. But here we are also being instructed to take happiness to the path because it creates so many obstacles for our practice. It is extremely difficult to take happiness to the path because we want it so much. We don't even perceive it as a problem.

This has been the case for Buddhist practitioners for ages. Things are difficult, so we practice. Things get better, and we forget the dharma. When things are better, we do not want to sit on the cushion. When things are better, we do not want to enter the shrine room. Our attachment to this "better samsara" is the cause of future suffering. We will inevitably fall back into the deep ocean of samsara, and our suffering will once again be vivid and intense. We will finally realize that we have forgotten the dharma and try to pick it back up. This cycle happens all over the world to modern practitioners—it is called "on again, off again" practice.

Some of us have been doing this on again, off again dharma practice for twenty or thirty years—some for even longer. Nothing improves internally for us because we are still chasing after happiness and lack true renunciation. It can be helpful to remember that having things go our way harms us as a practitioner. We are better off facing the adversity of samsara and deepening our renunciation.

When things are going well, don't forget the dharma! In Tibet we say, "That's the time you need to tighten your belt." When we are hungry and don't have enough to eat, we need to tighten our belt and have the discipline to get through it. If we think we need discipline when things are rough, we need even more discipline when things are going well. Maybe life is the best it has even been—our job is going well, family relationships are harmonious, and our lover feels like our soulmate. On one hand, it is not our fault that we want to take a break from practice when things are going well.

Who wants to sit on the cushion and face our own internal drama? But if we gain certainty in the suffering of samsara, realizing that our present happiness is just like a poisonous fruit, we can do it. We can remind ourselves, "It doesn't matter what circumstances or situation I am facing right now; it is still samsara." Remember that fire is hot. It burns. No matter what we touch in samsara, it will burn us. That's the nature of the life we have. We need to see this and accept it.

The great masters I met and connected with during my life really taught me this. They smiled when they saw changes happening in life, even very difficult ones. They spoke of being imprisoned during the Cultural Revolution in Tibet, saying, "Mao? Oh yes, we experienced that. Compared with that time, this situation I'm facing now is okay. It is the nature of samsara." They trained their minds and emotions to automatically improve their renunciation.

Gampopa also said, "Obstacles are the cause for applying the dharma." How wonderful it would be if we could see all of the obstacles and enemies in life as our lama and immediately work on our dharma practice. If we could all think in this way, the world would be emptied of ordinary beings and full of buddhas.

Advice for Not Being Depressed by Renunciation

What do we normally do when we are overwhelmed by our certainty in the suffering of samsara? Often we don't allow renunciation to arise and use that to practice the dharma. Instead, most people just let themselves get depressed. We may get involved in destructive emotional patterns or behaviors. We may try to disconnect and distance ourselves from the suffering of life. Or maybe we even become so tired of the life we live that we indulge in drugs, alcohol, sex, or other addictions. We do whatever we can to try to find peace and joy without realizing that we are just falling deeper into the cycle of samsara.

Reading the biographies of great masters can engender a deep sense of devotion, which can help us find greater enthusiasm to cut through the root of samsara through the mind of renunciation and genuine dharma practice. I read many biographies when I was younger, prompted by advice from my lama. One time, I was with my lama who was teaching on Atiyoga Dzogchen for one hundred days in a remote place far away from our shedra. Only a few students were there. After the teaching finished, we were supposed to go to my village. When the teachings were done, we needed to find a truck to travel across Tibet—one of those big Chinese flatbed trucks. My lama would sit up front with the driver, and we students would jump into the back. But barely any trucks ever came by that area.

Every day we waited and waited for a truck to come by. Whenever I heard a vehicle, I would run out to check if it was the right truck. I was homesick, and I couldn't wait to go home. I loved my parents and my brother so much, and I missed them terribly. Seeing my distress, one day my lama told me to read the life story of Buddha Shakyamuni. He gave me a huge volume that was about one thousand pages long. As I read it, I forgot about my homesickness. I was supposed to be cooking for my lama, but sometimes I even forgot to cook. My lama didn't care—he was so happy that he cooked instead. He would say, "Son, come have lunch," and I would realize that I had forgotten to cook the meal. When I saw my lama, my eyes would be red from crying because the story was so wonderful and inspiring. He was happy to see that. A month or two passed this way, and the time went by so fast.

After I finished that book, my lama told me to read the biographies of Tilopa, Naropa, and Milarepa. I had already memorized Milarepa's biography when I was younger, but I read it again. Reading these biographies again inspired me and generated in me deep devotion. When you are tired of samsara and all of its suffering, instead of getting depressed, I suggest reading the biographies of the masters. They inspire you, connect you to the dharma, and bring extraordinary blessings.

The benefit of reading biographies is they can show us a different way to handle life's suffering. These masters were so committed to the dharma because they saw the faults of ordinary life and samsara. From that realization they developed strong renunciation. We all know that fire burns. No one needs to put their hand into a burning flame to find out what will happen when our hand touches the flame. Incredibly, these realized masters developed an irreversible certainty that samsara is like a burning fire, where not even temporary happiness can be found. That's why they were able to commit to the genuine dharma, practice diligently, and take on so many hardships for the sake of realization.

Gampopa's Second Dharma

Grant your blessing so that my mind may turn toward the dharma.
Grant your blessing so that dharma may progress along the path.
Grant your blessing so that the path may clarify confusion.
Grant your blessing so that confusion may dawn as wisdom.

The second line of Gampopa's *Four Dharmas* says, "Grant your blessing so that dharma may progress along the path." Like the first line, Gampopa's second line is in the form of a prayer. After having reflected on the difficulty of cutting through attachment to samsara, it makes sense that Gampopa makes the heartfelt wish for our dharma practice to increase and progress along the path. Progressing along the path of dharma requires certainty in the nature of samsara. This certainty is the mind of renunciation itself, as Sakya Drakpa Gyaltsen referred to in the second attachment. It is the gateway to the dharma and the very source of genuine dharma practice.

What would it mean if we said the opposite, that dharma didn't follow the path? It would mean that even though we are trying to practice dharma and making a lot of effort with our body, speech, and mind, our dharma practice is not pure. It is colored by our attachment to samsara—all of the distractions in ordinary life that pull us off course. On the other hand, if we have renunciation and begin to cut through our attachment to samsara, dharma will certainly follow the path because there is no attachment to distract us. Our mind will not be pulled off the path and will remain focused on and attentive to what we are doing. By reversing our attachment to samsara, we will be able to generate renunciation, and this ensures that our practice will progress.

Making the prayer that dharma may follow the path may evoke the blessings of a realized master like Gampopa, but if we lack renunciation, these blessings won't be of much help. Making a prayer isn't going to be enough to make our dharma practice transformative. For this we need to develop certainty that the nature of samsara is suffering. Then, by relying on the mind of renunciation, dharma will follow the path naturally. All the other elements that support our dharma practice, such as studying with a lama, developing discipline, having a daily practice, cultivating diligence—all of these will simply be additional supportive conditions that ensure that dharma follows the path.

If we recite Gampopa's prayer by mouthing the words rotely, but we don't have devotion and we are not reflecting on the faults of samsara, then our prayer will not be a supportive condition to ensure that dharma follows the path. Making prayers is powerful when they are supported by a devoted mind and positive actions, but simply reciting the words of a prayer won't cause a major transformation on its own.

The best way to cut through our attachment to samsara and cultivate renunciation is to reflect on the faults of samsara over and over again. We should reflect on the faults of samsara so much that we stop seeing the possibility of a better samsara. This is something we should reflect on deeply. When we are getting what we want, is samsara really better? In what way does this help us? According to Gampopa's advice given earlier, the better the samsara seems, the worse it actually is! Renunciation isn't a quality that arises just by saying "I have renunciation" and snapping our fingers like magic. We have to stop seeing good qualities in samsara in order to give rise to that state of mind.

The attachment we have to samsara and ordinary life is the obstacle to entering and progressing along the genuine path of dharma. When we fail to put enough effort into cultivating the mind of renunciation, we cannot view our suffering as a spiritual guide. There is great benefit to seeing suffering as a spiritual guide because we can relate to it in a completely different way. Rather than simply trying to get through our suffering and not getting too upset and unbalanced in the process, we can see it as instructive and transformative. Our suffering can reveal our weaknesses and point out what qualities we still need to develop. It can help us relate to others with greater compassion and humility. It can also raze feelings of arrogance to the ground as we recognize our own humanity. If we don't see it this way, delving into our own suffering means that whatever we face is just going to cause more afflictive emotions, which will bring about more and more suffering. When we're faced with a barrage of suffering, how will we follow the path of dharma? This is even more reason to make the heartfelt wish that dharma progress along the path.

The many different sufferings of life are obstacles to accomplishing the dharma if they become distractions. It is only by seeing our suffering as the cause for renunciation and as the embodiment of our spiritual teacher that we can remove ourselves from the habit of being victimized by it. Suffering can assist us on the path of dharma like a friend instead of an enemy—and if we truly wish for our dharma practice to progress, we should warm up to it.

We should also examine ourselves to find out how much renunciation we actually have. We Tibetans say, "Only you truly know yourself." This means that those looking at us from the outside can't really know what good qualities and faults we have. But we can look inward and see what is really there and what is lacking. When we look inward, it does not make any sense to deceive ourselves.

All people, even dharma practitioners, are extremely attached to samsara and ordinary life. We should not fool ourselves thinking that we have cultivated deep renunciation if we have not. If our renunciation is strong, then we will not let ourselves waste even one single day by not practicing. We will make an effort at dharma practice moment by moment, watching our thoughts, recalling what we have been taught, and applying those instructions. Thoughts are invisible, and we are often unaware of our own thought patterns. Without moment-by-moment introspection, we may not realize how many unhealthy thoughts we have in a day.

Some people have asked me if dharma practitioners become cold and distant as a result of developing renunciation. This is a misunderstanding of the meaning "to reject." When we have genuine renunciation, our love toward others becomes more sincere. Inside, we know it's samsara. We know we are suffering and that everything is just temporary. But we also recognize we are together now, and this may not continue tomorrow, so we cherish it.

A Meaning-Based Commentary on the Second Attachment

When we examine the meaning of the first two lines of the quotation together, we can see how to move naturally from the meaning of the first line to the second line. Again, the first line says, "If you are attached to this life, you are not a dharma practitioner." If we don't separate from the cares of this life, we cannot practice the dharma authentically—in other words, the mind cannot follow the dharma. Even though we hear the meaning of the dharma and see the way others practice the dharma, our mind cannot truly understand how to follow the dharma because it is distracted and following something else. Or we could say that the mind cannot follow the dharma because we are too invested in this life.

Then, as Atisha's earlier quotation implies, if we can separate ourselves from the cares of this life, the mind will be able to follow the dharma. This is an extremely important point. Until we understand this and try to reduce our attachment to the cares of this life, we cannot move on to other aspects of practice. Because the mind cannot follow the dharma, our efforts at practice are fruitless and wasted.

As we begin to send the cares of this life from the mind, we see the benefit of lessening the attachment we have to ourselves as well as to everyone and everything around us. At this point, we should remind ourselves what it means to be less attached to this life. Some translators of the dharma choose to translate the phrase "cutting through attachment" as "detached." The word *detached* really does sound like a cold and distant state of mind. I would encourage practitioners not to think this way. Cutting through attachment simply means that we will slowly reverse the strong belief that all the different parts of ordinary life can bring lasting happiness. Seeing how much others are suffering due to this same way of thinking and believing is a source of compassion. If we find ourselves distancing ourselves from others because of our practice, we should seek guidance to find the error in our approach.

Once we begin to change the way we relate to this life, it becomes easier to contemplate the nature of samsara in the second line, "If you are attached to samsara, you do not have renunciation." We have already begun to see that attachment is the true cause of suffering. We may not think of ourselves as having many attachments at all, or we may think that our attachments aren't that deep and that they are more like preferences. But our attachment goes far beyond the microcosm of this life. We took birth in samsara this lifetime due to having self-attachment. This means that from lifetime to lifetime, we have always believed in a truly existent self. We protected it and tried to make ourselves happy in many selfish ways. This caused harm to others, thereby accumulating negative karma, which made sure that we kept being reborn in samsara in the future. We suffered when we didn't get what we wanted, experienced sadness or anger when we had conflicts or separated from loved ones, and faced pervasive, all-encompassing loss at the moment of death in each of those lifetimes.

We suffered over and over again in every lifetime, in very similar ways to the way we are suffering in this life because of the attachment generated by the mind. Thus, we can say that all our lifetimes have been characterized by attachment. This attachment touched everything: the things we liked and things we disliked, the wanted things and unwanted things. Whether we had a positive, negative, or neutral attachment, attachment has always been our main form of connection. From this attachment comes the three types of suffering: the suffering of change, when things cannot remain the way they are right now; the suffering of suffering, when we experience physical, emotional, and mental suffering all heaped upon each other; and all-pervasive suffering, where all beings in samsara are suffering and none is excluded.

Samsara itself is made up of countless versions of "this life." We have taken rebirth as countless versions of the person we are now. In every one of those lifetimes we experienced the sufferings of birth, aging, sickness, and death. We loved, hated, despaired, felt joy and sorrow, and had hopes and fears just as we do now. Then we died and the whole cycle started all over again. The only way to ensure that we do not do the same thing again is to develop renunciation.

Developing genuine renunciation means we start to gradually cut through some of the attachment we have to samsara and our ordinary ways of thinking. For example, as ordinary beings we place all our hopes for happiness on things or people outside ourselves. As an example, we may think that our spouse should not express anger toward us, and we are upset by their angry words. In response to their anger, we feel bad, and then we blame our bad feelings on them. This is a normal way of thinking about others, especially when we hold the belief that there is a better version of samsara in which outside people and situations can make us happy.

A practitioner who has developed some renunciation and has contemplated the nature of samsara thinks about this same occurrence a bit differently. It sounds something like, "My spouse just behaves the way they do because they are experiencing their karma, which causes them to express a lot of anger. Rather than getting upset, I should try to take care of my own emotional reaction because my emotional reaction causes both of us suffering, and it also escalates the conflict between us. If I am angry, I should try to practice patience. If I am disappointed, I should try to reflect on the nature of samsara, where happiness can never be found." When we have renunciation, we can gradually start to cut through our ordinary way of thinking, which enables us to take dharma to the path.

All obstacles on the path of dharma are created by our attachment to samsara. Once we gradually cut through our attachment to samsara, these obstacles vanish because there is nothing stopping us from applying the dharma just the way that it's taught. However much we can cut through our attachment to samsara, the dharma we practice and understand becomes more and more genuine, rather than having our own ideas overlaid and superimposed upon it.

When we are not working at cutting through our attachment to samsara, all the dharma we practice is just a facade. We may recite prayers or mantra or engage in some kind of traditional practice, but when we are doing it based on our attachment to samsara, the dharma we practice is not genuine. We are just going through the motions.

To take dharma to the path, we need to be willing to look at and see the faults of samsara. This may be something we find depressing or difficult to do, but when we experience disappointment with the nature of samsara, we need to find the cause of that disappointment. Is that disappointment really coming from the outside? In other words, are we disappointed because something went wrong and didn't turn out the right way—the way we think it should have? Or are we disappointed because we are attached to a certain expectation or hope about how things should have turned out? Are we disappointed because we are attached to samsara being different—better—than it actually is? Or are we disappointed by our inability to see the nature of samsara as it is, which is the true cause of our suffering? Is it the thing on the outside or what's happening in our mind on the inside? If we truly believe that we are the creator of our own suffering, then based on dharma practice, we can liberate ourselves from that suffering.

What Does It Mean to Say We Create Our Own Suffering?

This essential topic in the lojong teachings is both misunderstood by Western audiences and difficult to swallow. Traditionally, all masters of the lojong tradition train in this idea: suffering is the natural consequence of self-attachment; when we suffer, there is no use looking on the outside for someone or something to blame. Rather, if we look in the mirror and see the way in which our own self-attachment has caused us problems, we can apply the dharma and slowly retrain the mind not to repeat these kinds of painful habits. This is the essence of mind training. Shantideva's *Way of the Bodhisattva* is composed of one thousand verses in ten chapters, and every verse in every single chapter presents a way to help us accept that we are the creators of our own suffering and to apply the lojong teachings to the mind. This way of thinking and style of practice is the very essence of the lojong tradition.

To the Western ear, this idea can sound very different than it does to a Tibetan. In Tibetan culture, we don't tend toward self-hatred, so when we say that we are the creators of our own suffering, there is no danger of using that idea to berate or punish ourselves. I always caution students about this when they start to train in the lojong teachings seriously. Lojong gives us the method to purify and change past negative habits, which will allow us to become a kinder and more compassionate person. This compassion extends both within and without. If we find that the way we apply the lojong teachings is taking on the character of negative "self-harm," we need to step back and get clarification from our spiritual guide.

"Self-harm" can have both positive and negative meanings. The negative meaning is to use the dharma to beat ourselves up. The positive approach is to use the lojong teachings to *harm our self-attachment*, to start to wear it down so that our emotional reactions aren't so strong and we can begin to cut through our attachments to this life and samsara. This type of practice brings joy and happiness to us and those around us, which makes it easy to see when we are doing it right.

This positive meaning of harming our self-attachment is quite radical if we really contemplate it. To do this, we have to deal a blow to our ordinary belief system. We have to be willing to think, "I am unhappy with what is happening right now, but my unhappiness is actually caused by me—my wishes, my expectations, my hopes, my attachments," and so on. It's not "my fault" in the traditional sense of casting blame at ourselves; but yet it is the sobering thought that "I am suffering because of the deep attachment I have to myself and what I want for myself."

We perpetuate our own suffering in a variety of ways—that is, engage in self-harm according to the dharma. Sometimes we suffer because we choose to believe that life is different than it is. If we invest in false beliefs—such as "My parents are always going to be there for me, I'm always going to have everything I need, I'm going to be healthy, things will always get better"— then we are planting the seeds for future suffering. Temporarily believing in these ideas may make us feel better for a while, but sooner or later we will have to face change and loss, whether we like it or not.

Another way we create suffering is by trying to micromanage our experience rather than transform it through lojong practice. We may try to make things the way we think they should be to avoid feeling disappointed by how life actually is. We may wear rose-colored glasses to see things in a good light. This can be a positive way to see the world, but not if we are blind to the fact that our optimism doesn't change the nature of samsara—it just makes it a bit easier to tolerate and work with in the moment.

There is a catchphrase in the dharma: "Be present." People also use it in contexts other than the dharma. But when we are talking about being the creators of our own suffering, this catchphrase is a very helpful thing to think about. Some of the suffering we experience happens because we are unable to distinguish between the past and the present. We may think something like, "I don't agree with the teaching that I create my own suffering. I had this terrible thing happen in the past. It was painful and I did not create it."

A lojong practitioner thinks about this differently. We would say that even though some difficult karma ripened, we suffered when we experienced it, and now that experience is over. It occurred in the past and is no longer occurring. Most of us, however, insist on bringing that painful past experience into the present and obsessing about it or recreating it. This is the way of humans—we just recycle our past suffering and bring it into the present. The past experience of suffering then defines the experience we are having right now. Our pain never dulls or gets old because we constantly relive it. Especially in Western culture, we invite a lot of suffering to ourselves by not leaving the past in the past.

From this point of view, the idea of "being present" is very profound and deserves some thought. How much time do we lose by getting lost in the past, and how much unhappiness do we create for ourselves by choosing to follow this emotional pattern? If we are trying to free up our minds to practice the dharma, it is important to consider where our mental and emotional energy is tied up.

If we are not able to see ourselves as the creator of our own suffering, there will be two results. The first is that our experience in samsara will be the same or worse than it is now. What we experience now in samsara is due to the habitual tendencies we have already developed. We could just continue the way we are and things would seem mostly the same. But usually what happens is that when we encounter the habit, we make it stronger. We keep acting out the habit in a cyclic way, and it gradually builds up. When our habits become stronger, we suffer more.

The second result is that based on our own behavior and strong emotions, we become the reason people around us experience unhappiness. This is logical. When we are unhappy or reacting emotionally in some way, the people around us either feel our energy or are faced with our unhappy, angry, or intolerant words or disposition. When we do not take responsibility for our own suffering, not only does our own unhappiness intensify but so does that of others around us. To cut through our attachment to samsara, then, we must know its nature. And knowing its nature, we must generate renunciation. That is why Patrul Rinpoche said, "The gateway to the path of liberation is renunciation."

Ask yourself, "Do I really, truly have renunciation?" It is an extremely difficult state of mind to achieve, and even if you achieve it once, it is difficult to maintain. If you find that you lack it, keep in mind that this will be the biggest obstacle to maintaining a lifelong dharma practice. Lacking renunciation is a universal thing. It happens a lot of the time in Western Buddhist communities, and these days even happens to Tibetans. It's hard to find a practitioner who has renunciation.

Milarepa, one of Tibet's most famous yogis and poets, set a powerful example of renunciation. He committed many harmful actions and harmed many beings. But because of his renunciation, in addition to his diligence, he accomplished Mahamudra practice* in one lifetime. Reading his biography and that of other masters can be extremely helpful. Most of us probably have no idea how great yogis practiced and what they were like. When we don't know how they practiced, it is difficult to understand how we could possibly emulate their example.

It can be useful to read the biographies of the masters from all four schools of Tibetan Buddhism. You could read more about the life of Sakya Drakpa Gyaltsen, the author of this verse, and Gampopa, the great Kagyu master. In addition to Milarepa, it is essential to read the biographies of Tilopa, Naropa, and Marpa. What incredible practitioners! We can read about the life of Je Tsongkapa, who accumulated a vast amount of merit during his lifetime, which led him to the state of being a realized master. And Longchenpa's and Jigme Lingpa's biographies detail the hardships that these masters undertook to realize Atiyoga Dzogchen. Based on renunciation, all of these masters achieved realization in one lifetime.

An incredible example of devotional diligence can be found in the story of the life and realization of Yeshe Tsogyal. If we can emulate Yeshe Tsogyal's capacity to practice and face hardship and austerity, we are truly an authentic practitioner. Or we could read Tara's biography, which details how she generated aspirational bodhicitta, and how she made such a vast aspiration to benefit beings because of seeing the faults of samsara. Her level of renunciation was incredible.

---

* Mahamudra is the pinnacle practice according to the Kagyu school of Vajrayana Buddhism.

I am not advising that we should constantly think about the faults of samsara and make ourselves depressed. Instead, here is how you can use the technique. If your partner is being really nasty to you today, you can say to yourself, "I live in samsara. Things will change in a moment if I can be patient enough to wait it out." If things aren't going your way, you can say to yourself, "My life is crap. Oh, okay—it's samsara. Samsara is crap, so I am experiencing crap. No problem. I have the dharma to get me through it." When someone is kind to you, you can rejoice and then think, "I must remember I'm in samsara, and people won't be nice to me all the time." When you see someone who is happy, you can think, "I rejoice with them! But we are in samsara, so I will also remember that no happiness can last." When you have a good day, don't think, "Today I don't need the dharma." Instead, think, "Oh, yes, samsara is a roller coaster. It can go up, and it will go back down." If your family life is great, you should think, "How wonderful! But I will not expect it to be like this forever. Problems will eventually surface." That's how we use this teaching to train the mind.

Even if we feel hurt because a person close to us is being unkind or they are difficult to be around, we can find a way to empathize with what they are facing in samsara. We can think about what is going on for that person and say to ourselves, "Oh, wow, they are suffering a lot right now." Even if we aren't sure what exactly is happening, since we are aware of how much we suffer every day, we can imagine it is the same for them. None of us is getting exactly what we want, and we are all facing loss and separation.

We can also reflect on how when others don't practice the dharma, they don't realize that they are creating their own suffering and have no way to get out of this pattern. It is without beginning and without end for them. Unless they interrupt the cycle of samsara through the practice of the genuine dharma, we can project with certainty that things in the future will be like they are now, without any fundamental change. When we feel hurt by others, it is helpful to think, "We are all suffering from ignorance and confusion that stems from self-attachment and attachment to samsara. Because of these attachments, we hurt others even without meaning to." There is a lot of fuel for compassion in this way of thinking.

Contemplating Death

Life in Western culture is like living in a god realm. According to the traditional Buddhist explanation, the god realms are characterized by abundant wealth, long life, and a fear of death that is so strong that the gods forget about it completely until it occurs. The West has fairly abundant wealth, and most of us avoid the merest thought of death. Even Vajrayana practitioners who have been practicing the dharma for forty years sometimes do not want to talk about death. Then when illness comes, we don't know what to do. When our loved ones die, we don't know what to do. We never thought about it before, and we don't want to think about it now. We avoid things like this because it is painful to acknowledge the nature of samsara.

Many people in this part of the world have never even witnessed a loved one dying because people die in hospitals or at home alone. Again, we shouldn't think about samsara so much that it depresses us. But we should use our knowledge of the nature of samsara to mature our hearts, minds, and dharma practice. That's what the lamas in Tibet say: "Samsara is manifesting. What else can we do but apply the dharma!" We can use everyday tragedies as conditions to push us to practice.

No matter how our life is right now, it is a reflection of the nature of samsara. We have this in common with everyone in the world—everyone around us is experiencing the suffering of samsara too. Almost no one thinks this way. When we suffer, we feel it is our suffering alone. It is difficult to realize that others are experiencing the same or similar suffering. What is the positive in all of this? If we have the dharma, we can apply it! We have a thousand chances to apply the dharma every day. The real samsara is here, in our own minds, and it manifests as an outside appearance. It is our own karma and our own karmic perception.

If we could think of samsara as being a manifestation of our own karma, this would be incredibly helpful. "This is my karma. I am experiencing it, and I have to deal with it. Therefore, I should work on practicing more and have more compassion for others." Our individual suffering and our karma are unique. We created the causes for suffering in the past, then we experienced the result of those actions as suffering. This is how cause and effect work. Our individual karma is caused by our individual habitual patterns. Until we see the suffering that we created as our personal spiritual guide, it will just keep increasing. The more we resist it, invest in it, or are unwilling to accept it, the stronger our habits (which are the causes of future suffering) get. These are all forms of attachment, and, as we know, attachment brings suffering. The most important thing we can do as a practitioner is focus on how to pacify ourselves using the lojong teachings to reduce our mental, emotional, and physical reactions. This is what lojong masters call "taming the mind."

By reacting less now, we reduce the cause of future suffering. With fewer causes of suffering, we will experience less suffering in the future. Our karma is our karma. We cannot change the karma we have accumulated in the past. But we can choose to apply the dharma in the present moment and to transform our own mental and emotional habits. Don't set the bar too high. Even small changes will slowly add up, just like drops of water slowly fill a bucket. If we apply the lojong teachings with consistency, personal transformation is not just possible but a certainty. Taking dharma to the path in this way, we will certainly reshape our future experiences, make it even easier for our dharma practice to gain momentum, and continue to follow the genuine path.

The Third Line

If you are attached to this life, you are not a dharma practitioner.
If you are attached to samsara, you do not have renunciation.
If you are attached to self-interest, you do not have bodhicitta.
If any grasping is present, it is not the view.

A Language-Based Commentary on the Third Attachment

The third line states, "If you are attached to self-interest, you do not have bodhicitta." Let's begin a close reading of this line by looking at the phrase "self-interest," or *bdag don* in Tibetan. *Don* can be translated as "interest" or "benefit." Reflecting on the difference between these two possible translations brings some additional richness to the meaning of this line.

For this translation, we have chosen to translate *bdag don* as "self-interest" because it more clearly reflects the tendency to work for ourself, our wishes, our dreams, and those we care about when we live in samsara. This is in direct contrast to how a practitioner behaves once they have entered the bodhisattva path and have generated aspirational bodhicitta. In fact, when we train in the mind of bodhicitta, we are taught to focus wholly on others and give up on trying to get what we want for ourselves. This is the opposite of self-interest, which means that we are invested in getting an advantage for ourselves, and in doing so, we disregard others.

A slightly different way of understanding "self-interest" is to more literally read it to mean "interest in myself," which illustrates the strong self-attachment and self-centeredness of ordinary beings. The word *interest* also sounds pragmatic and financially driven, in contrast to the word *benefit*, which is often used in the dharma to discuss bodhisattva activity.

However, considering the possibility of using the word *benefit* in the same line adds to its meaning. A self-interested practitioner doesn't have any intention to give up what they want for others' benefit. A self-absorbed or self-centered practitioner cannot work for others' benefit, so we can be sure that they have not been able to give rise to bodhicitta. These ideas help clarify the statement being made.

Some Advice on Self-Cherishing from the Kadam Masters of Old
Atisha's master, the mahasiddha* Jowo Serlingpa, said,

> "I" is the root of all negative karma,
> Something that should be flung far away.
> Others are the source of enlightenment.
> Bind them to yourself and keep them close.

The first line states that "I" is the root of negative karma because, based on self-grasping and self-cherishing, we label the self "I" even though no lasting and permanent "I" truly exists. Once we realize that the self we call "I" is the cause of our negative karma (which is the cause of our suffering in the past, present, and future), we should relinquish our attachment to it completely and keep our distance from it as much as possible. Even better, we should throw it away just like trash! If we truly develop conviction in the nature of karma and begin to trust that we will inevitably experience the result of the karma we accumulate, we will find that giving up our self-cherishing and self-interest is not as difficult as we think.

In this spirit, Atisha said we should discard self-cherishing just like our father's corpse. No matter how much we love our father when he is alive, once he has passed away, we feel no hesitation

---

* A mahasiddha is an individual who, through Vajrayana practice, attains the realization of siddhis—realization and the manifestation of spiritual abilities, clairvoyance, and powers.

to discard his rotting corpse. In Tibet, we often keep the corpse of a loved one for three days for spiritual purposes, but in the modern West, we usually just leave a loved one's corpse in the hospital or morgue and don't even bring them home. Just so, we should discard our self-cherishing, which is the cause of all suffering, and focus on training the mind in bodhicitta, the source of all happiness.

In this same light, the famous Kadam master Geshe Langri Thangba said, "No matter what profound teaching I review among the sutra and tantra, all faults come from self-cherishing. All good qualities come from other sentient beings. Therefore, give all profit and victory to others and take all loss and defeat upon yourself."

Further Clarification from Longchenpa

In *A Mirror Revealing the Crucial Points, Advice on the Ultimate Meaning*, Longchenpa describes the meaning of self-interest by saying, "If you are not free of attachment and anger, you cannot embody the Mahayana." He uses the words "attachment and anger" instead of "self-interest." We may not have ever thought of emotions such as attachment (sometimes also translated as "desire" or "passion") and anger as being signs of self-interest. Most of us who have an intimate connection with our emotions see them as sources of real and true information about the world— we don't think of them as showing our self-interest. Instead, we may see our emotions are something that we rely upon to express ourselves and make decisions. They allow us to navigate a complicated world and have complicated relationships without getting hurt too much in the process. It can seem like our emotions accompany us through our hard times and are more reliable than even our closest friends. We say things like, "I need to sort out how I feel" or "Let me sit with how I feel" to make sense of life.

This reflects the belief many of us have that our emotions can give us needed feedback to help us figure out what we should do next.

A lojong practitioner has a much different relationship with their emotions. Because we have spent time contemplating and reflecting on the idea that attachment to this life and samsara brings suffering, and if we have begun to have some certainty that the nature of samsara is suffering, we need not put so much weight on our emotions. From the point of view of the dharma, emotions are nothing more than reactions that occur based on the degree of attachment we have to this life and samsara as a whole.

How do we understand emotions as being a sign of self-interest? Let's say someone criticizes us and we react with a feeling of anger. We might think what they said is unfair and unjust, or maybe even that what they said is true but saying it out loud is unkind or embarrassing. Our anger arises out of self-attachment and a feeling of self-interest—we want to protect ourselves or preserve our good name or the image that we see or is seen by others. We also may want to use our anger to stop the other person from criticizing us again. This self-protective feeling gets stronger when unwanted situations occur because it seems like things are going downhill and we are losing our advantage.

How would a person with no self-interest respond? My root lama or Lama Tsepel, because these masters had no self-attachment, genuinely wouldn't care if anyone criticized them. They would also feel grateful for the opportunity to see any latent self-attachment arise so that it could be further cut down.

This attitude of genuinely not caring is different from acting like we don't care. In Western culture, one way we often cope with being criticized by others is to act like we don't care what anyone thinks about us. But this feeling is still a reaction to the situation—it is still an afflictive emotion that is laden with self-attachment. We can tell because it is accompanied by other emotions, such as feelings of defiance, coldness, or indifference. This is definitely not bodhicitta.

Bodhicitta not only lacks self-interest but is completely engulfed by the energy of loving-kindness and compassion. We care about the well-being of everyone and everything. No matter how they treat us, we are full of loving warmth, and people feel that warmth when they meet us. This is the mindset of a realized master.

Why did Longchenpa say that we can't embody the Mahayana if we have anger and attachment? This has to do with the defining characteristics of being a Mahayana Buddhist. Entering the Mahayana means that we have taken the bodhisattva vow and have begun training in aspirational bodhicitta. When we take the bodhisattva vow, we promise to train in aspiration and engaged bodhicitta in the same way as the bodhisattvas of the past. For these realized bodhisattvas, bodhicitta is a state of realization that is completely free from self-attachment. Because that bodhisattva has realized the empty nature of their own self and their corporeal body, they have nothing to protect, nothing to defend, nothing to be angry about, and no passion or ordinary desire. In other words, there is no self-interest in this state because there is no self to be interested in. And due to having trained in bodhicitta on the path, they have already habituated themselves to solely focusing on the benefit of others.

This is very different from what happens for an ordinary practitioner. Many of us have taken the bodhisattva vow, but we still feel attachment and anger every day, sometimes very intensely. But if we take up the path of lojong, we have to question if this is really where we want to continue investing our time and energy. For a lojong practitioner, the outlook is always long term—we are always asking, for example, "Does tolerating this difficulty now benefit my dharma practice in the future?" or "Is the way I'm handling this going to bring peace and happiness to myself and others now and in the future?"

When Longchenpa explains that when we experience strong emotions (attachment and anger) we cannot "embody" the

Mahayana, his words don't mean that we can't enter the Mahayana path. Rather, he means we cannot keep our bodhicitta when we are emotional and self-centered. This is a useful clarification. None of us should feel like we aren't good enough to train in the Mahayana just because we have ordinary emotions and self-attachment. However, we should also understand that realizing the ultimate nature of bodhicitta—which is the realization of all buddhas and bodhisattvas—is not possible when we go back to our ordinary habitual ways of thinking and approaching life. We must gradually purify the mind's selfishness and retrain ourselves by taking up the bodhisattva path.

We cannot embody the dharma if we are constantly worried about ourselves, what we want, and how others should treat us. That is why all the great lojong masters gave the advice to "look in the mirror." We must stop trying to pacify our attachment and anger by looking outside of ourselves for someone or something to blame. Instead, we should look in the mirror—at ourselves. How are the emotions we are experiencing caused by our own self-interest?

Some Wisdom from Shantideva

Having stepped onto the path of lojong practice, we have faced—or will soon face—the question of how to find long-term happiness. Do we find happiness based on trying to get what we want, trying to assert our own self-interest? According to the dharma, the harder we try to get what we want, the more unhappy we become. In *Way of the Bodhisattva*, Shantideva explained it like this:

> All the joy the world contains
> Has come through wishing happiness for others.
> All the misery the world contains
> Has come through wanting pleasure for oneself.

Is there need for lengthy explanation?
Childish beings look out for themselves;
Buddhas labor for the good of others:
See the difference that divides them!*

These verses get to the very heart of the lojong teachings and the problem with self-interest. When we react with attachment or anger, we may think that we are protecting ourselves and preserving our self-interest by making sure that we are okay, comfortable, or in control. But this very act of self-protection simply reinforces the self-attachment that has been causing our suffering to begin with.

If we truly wish to cultivate the mind of bodhicitta, we must contemplate the meaning of these verses deeply. Is it really possible that the way we have been trying to find happiness our whole lives is wrong? It is not only us who have been striving constantly in our own self-interest, but also everyone around us, including our parents, teachers, and elders—the people who we look up to the most. Even if we have moments where we believe that what Shantideva says is true, we are likely to forget it once whatever painful experience we are having begins to subside. This is the basic habit of self-attachment, so we should not be easily discouraged or feel we aren't making much progress, even if we attempt to reverse the way we think many times. We are bound to fail, but there will also be moments where we see things clearly and build up our certainty that working for the benefit of others is what brings the most joy.

If we contemplate Shantideva's words and use them as the ground for our practice, we can start to gain more confidence. We can examine each situation as it comes up. For example, the harder

---

* Shantideva, *The Way of the Bodhisattva*, trans. Padmakara Translation Group (Boston: Shambhala, 2008), 214.

we try to make others do what we want—setting high expectations for them and hoping that they'll meet them—the more our relationships will be strained. The more we offer unconditional love and support to others, the more ease and laughter we will have with others. In the long term, having an ordinary level of confidence that the cause of happiness is benefiting others will not be sufficient. We need extraordinary confidence because when we are on the bodhisattva path, we will face myriad trials and difficulties, especially as we try to give up more and more of our self-attachment. In every one of those situations, we will need to stick with the bodhisattva path, not react with attachment and anger, and give up on our feelings of self-interest. As lojong practitioners, we must have an extremely deep conviction in Shantideva's words and take them as the very premise for why we practice the dharma.

When we "see the difference that divides" Buddhas from ordinary beings, we can be inspired and motivated to emulate the way that they practiced. After all, imitating the way ordinary beings act will only result in us remaining an ordinary being in the future. But if we follow the bodhisattva path, it is possible to transform the mind and give up all attachment and anger completely.

The Meaning of Bodhicitta

Let's turn our attention to the second half of the line from Sakya Drakpa Gyaltsen: "If you are attached to self-interest, you do not have bodhicitta." *Bodhicitta* is made up of four syllables in the original Tibetan: *byangchub kyi sems*. The first syllable, *byang*, means to "cleanse or purify." Bodhicitta, in its most genuine state, is stainless and wholly uncorrupted by self-attachment or attachment to the phenomenal world. It is unsullied by emotional, cognitive, or habitual obscurations or any other type of impurity. The second syllable, *chub*, means "consummate or perfect." Together, these two words mean "perfectly purified," but they are also translated as "enlightenment," "awakening," or "realization." Thus, realization or enlightenment itself is perfectly purified of any attachment, obscuration, or impurity whatsoever. The last two syllables, *kyi sems*, mean "mind of," so altogether, bodhicitta means "awakened mind," or "mind of enlightenment." We should note that bodhicitta is not some elementary stage of practice—its very core is realization itself. If we realized the nature of bodhicitta, we would be a realized master in league with all the buddhas and bodhisattvas of the past.

Does Bodhicitta Have Self-Interest?

Patrul Rinpoche said, "Based on training in bodhicitta, I cut through the habit of self-interest." My own root lama also often said it this way: "Bodhicitta cuts through the mind's obsession with self-interest." These quotations convey the idea that as human beings, we focus only on ourselves—how we feel, what we need, and how to keep getting what we need. In the face of this obsessive self-cherishing, it is difficult to think of what others need or how to help them. Even if we have made a concerted effort to change this tendency in ourselves, it is difficult to make much progress using ordinary methods. Luckily the tendency to self-cherish naturally diminishes when we train in bodhicitta.

Patrul Rinpoche clearly states that bodhicitta is devoid of any self-interest. Not only is bodhicitta free of self-interest but it is the very method for cutting through self-interest. How does this method work? It is somewhat difficult to understand before we try it. In the beginning, when we first hear about bodhicitta, we may feel some fear or alarm. From the outside, it may look like we are turning against ourselves. Rather than protecting ourselves from harm, we pay less attention to ourselves and turn our focus to others. A common reaction is "Aren't we just letting people walk all over us like a doormat?" I have heard this statement made by practitioners many times during the years I have lived in America. I don't think this characterization is correct. A practitioner who has firmly developed bodhicitta is willing to compromise, concede, and tolerate for the benefit of connections with others, to tame their own mind, or because the situation requires it. Because their motivation and actions are purposeful, they are a source of merit and spiritual growth. The experience is nothing like letting someone walk all over us.

On the other hand, to use this magical method of bodhicitta, we must go against the grain of our selfish mind completely. In the beginning, this is a very difficult idea to swallow. What is the method being used when we train the mind in bodhicitta? Simply put, we train the mind to focus on others, and we try to reduce the mind's obsession with ourselves. The modern world is characterized by extreme self-obsession, and it has resulted in high rates of mental illness, poor family relationships, strong feelings of animosity or violence between groups of people who disagree, poor self-image, self-hatred, and so on. You might wonder how all of these problems could be blamed on the mind's self-obsession. The answer is simple—when we are wrapped up in ourselves, we have no time or space to think of anyone else. Our attachment to this life and samsara becomes stronger and stronger, which creates stronger and stronger emotional reactions and mental and physical imbalances. Eventually, because the world looks the way it does as a result of our own karmic perception, we see a world filled with hatred, disagreements, and violence. This indicates that we lack positive feelings such as compassion, love, patience, tolerance, and joy. Strong self-attachment reduces our feelings of connection with others and heightens our emotional reactions such as impatience, irritation, and agitation. The modern world is full of beings just like this, many of whom have little to no spiritual life and are filled with misery and disappointment about the life they are living, just like we are.

Only a very radical method can turn the tables on this kind of downward spiral. When we grab hold of the mind of bodhicitta, we may initially do so out of desperation, without really wishing for others' benefit in our heart. We might have heard that training in this way can bring relief to the mind, and so in the beginning, we do it because nothing else we have tried has worked. We may have tried therapy, medications, diets, yoga, or other kinds of programs that promote well-being. We may cook nourishing food and take long, hot baths to try to feel better. These things may provide some relief, but they don't address the fundamental problem, which was introduced in the first two lines of *Parting from the Four Attachments*—the attachment we have to this life and samsara. If we engage in a normal method that keeps the focus on ourselves—trying to get ourselves to relax, for example, or trying to let go of past situations by analyzing and resolving them—there can be no fundamental change. We can't let go of self-obsession by focusing on the self. It simply won't work. Focusing on the self only strengthens our self-interest and magnifies what already hurts.

To let go of self-interest, we need a method that is both powerful and completely different from all the ordinary methods we have tried. It must be diamond hard to be able to cut through our deep habit of self-attachment. Bodhicitta, at least in Western culture, looks weak from the outside. How could simply focusing on the happiness of others create such a fundamental change in the heart and mind? It seems untenable. That's why I call it magical. Just like alchemy, it transforms the selfish heart inside of us into gold. Oh, the joy of not thinking of ourselves constantly! What a wonderful break from using the microscope to examine all the little things that bother us from moment to moment. This kind of relief is available to all of us, and it is not hard to obtain. We simply need the courage to start training the mind and take a leap of faith that giving up the habit of self-protection and self-interest is the path to inviting in joy and happiness.

Gampopa's Third Dharma

Grant your blessing so that my mind may turn toward the dharma.
Grant your blessing so that dharma may progress along the path.
Grant your blessing so that the path may clarify confusion.
Grant your blessing so that confusion may dawn as wisdom.

The third line of Gampopa's *Four Dharmas* says, "Grant your blessing so that the path may clarify confusion." Here, *confusion* could refer to a couple of different things. It might mean errors or mistakes that we make when we are on the path. For example, we might misunderstand the dharma and how the dharma works. As we have pointed out several times already, this is certainly the case for many modern practitioners.

Another reason we might experience confusion is if we don't find a suitable spiritual guide to help us enter the path properly and avoid the pitfalls and obstacles that keep our practice from developing. For example, we might not meet a qualified spiritual teacher who holds an unbroken Vajrayana lineage, so it is not possible to receive the proper lineage teachings. In this case, if the methods we rely upon to practice the dharma are themselves confused, we will not make much progress no matter how much effort we make.

Additionally, we make this prayer to clear up the confusion that many of us have about training the mind in bodhicitta. We might misunderstand the purpose of the training and think it is self-abating—in turning away from our own benefit, it may seem like we are being harsh or unkind to ourselves. This happens when we are confused about what really happens to a being who perfects the nature of bodhicitta—we don't realize that they become a fully realized master! We may think things like, "What will happen if I focus wholly on others? Who will care for me?" Because we live in a society where we must advocate for ourselves in many situations, we might wonder if training in bodhicitta means that we cannot stand up for ourselves. In modern Western society, we need a certain kind of pragmatic attitude to navigate everyday life. We may worry we would lose this entirely.

Certainly, we will change as a result of training the mind in bodhicitta. But the changes are positive and should not be considered a source of fear and anxiety. We must remember that our own attitude and mind will transform as a result of our mind training. We will become a person who has fewer cares and worries about themselves and has more space in their mind and heart for joy. Lama Tsepel is the perfect example of having trained the mind in bodhicitta to the level of a master. Because he trained his mind only to care for the welfare of others, he didn't have a single care for himself—this was reflected in what he ate and drank, what he wore, and where he lived. Because of our own self-attachment, we may not want to live the way Lama Tsepel did. But we should also be clear that his lack of self-interest and self-attachment didn't cause him any suffering. Having given these up, he was left with spiritual mastery, great confidence, and joy in living.

Reflecting on Lama Tsepel's example, we can recognize that even if we advocate for ourselves in certain necessary situations, or spend time on self-care, the attitude behind those actions can be different because of our dharma practice. We can see them as necessary actions to build our energy and strength for dharma practice, to help others in the best way we can, and continue taking the difficulties of life to the path. Even actions that look ordinary can be extraordinary if they have a great motivation like bodhicitta behind them.

To dispel confusion about how the dharma works, Gampopa left us some useful advice. In *Gampopa's Oral Advice: Precious Garland of the Supreme Path*, he said, "When you are a beginner on the path, listen to and contemplate the dharma. Make sure you understand the dharma, then apply the dharma." Here he reveals something more about the meaning of the prayer he made in the third line. If we take up the path properly, confusion will be dispelled—but if we fail to take up the path properly, our confusion will only get deeper. Along with making prayers and aspirations, we should receive authentic dharma teachings from a qualified teacher and reflect on their meaning. It is essential that we know who we are receiving dharma teachings from and that we take time to examine that person and their qualifications.

After we receive teachings from such a master, we should make sure we understand what we have been taught. If we reflect on the meaning and are confused, we should ask questions to clear up our confusion. Especially when training in bodhicitta, the very essence of the path, it is essential we understand how to apply the teachings properly.

From time to time, practitioners who misunderstand the lojong teachings use their practice in a harmful way. This is also a kind of confusion. For example, when we practice lojong, the target is our self-attachment. We are attempting to use the teachings to break down our self-attachment and identity—not because who we are is inherently bad but rather the habitual way we do things is causing us so much suffering. Sometimes practitioners experience confusion and don't target their self-attachment. They use lojong to punish themselves with self-hatred, criticism, or anger. We should be clear that the lojong teachings do not contain such methods. In fact, using the teachings in this way is contrary to their purpose. This is just the same old pattern of self-obsession and making ourselves the center of the world. In misusing the lojong teachings this way, we are creating and prolonging our own suffering.

There are no ordinary, worldly methods to break down self-attachment. When it comes to self-attachment, the methods of samsara only build it up. This is because ordinary people misunderstand what the source of happiness is. It seems counterintuitive to think that giving up on trying to get what we want could actually bring us happiness. It is so simple that most of us can't believe it, and even if we think it is true, we are too afraid to try. Shantideva expressed this in *Way of the Bodhisattva*:

> If I do not interchange
> My happiness for others' pain,
> Enlightenment will never be attained,
> And even in samsara, joy will fly from me.*

A Meaning-Based Commentary on the Third Attachment

To fully understand the meaning of the Sakya Drakpa Gyaltsen's third line, it is helpful to closely read the second and third lines together to see how the meaning of the third line builds upon the second.

> If you are attached to samsara, you do not have renunciation.
> If you are attached to self-interest, you do not have bodhicitta.

In the second line, the key point is when we see samsara clearly, we develop a mind of renunciation. Because our vision has finally cleared up, we are no longer confused about the source of happiness—in other words, we no longer expect that we will be able to get happiness from within samsara, just like we will never be able to squeeze butter from sand. Or maybe we should say that our vision has cleared up temporarily. It would be wonderful if renunciation was something that, once we experienced it, was constantly present within the mind. Unfortunately, renunciation

---

* Shantideva, *The Way of the Bodhisattva*, trans. Padmakara Translation Group (Boston: Shambhala, 2008), 214.

is something we have to continually strive for. It is a quality that waxes and wanes based on our certainty in the nature of samsara.

At times we may feel profound certainty and conviction that the nature of samsara is suffering. At other times, as we look at the different situations we face, we might mistakenly think that with just the right amount of ingenuity, things will turn out the way we want. It is good to remember that renunciation has within it the best possible kind of hopelessness. Once we are certain about the nature of samsara, we can relax and give up all hope that it is going to make us happy. However, this kind of hopelessness can be difficult to bear. Once we experience it, if we don't have enough conviction in the dharma, we are in danger of becoming overwhelmed or depressed.

The lineage masters set the example of combining the mind of renunciation with an unwavering determination to practice the dharma. Without their courage and strength of mind, this can be a difficult example to follow. Often what happens to ordinary beings like us is that we can't tolerate the idea that samsara is hopeless. We don't truly want to give up on the idea that ordinary life can make us happy. Instead of applying the dharma, we go back to our habitual pattern of attachment to samsara, believing it is going to be different this time.

It is not easy to develop the mind of renunciation firmly. It takes so much effort on our part to gradually apply the dharma to ourselves and to see all of the myriad ways that we are still invested in life in samsara, despite our best efforts to enter the path of dharma. As we work at making our renunciation more and more stable and try to bring it into the mind more often, we will begin to turn away from samsara and put more focus on the dharma. This is what the teachings call "turning the mind toward the dharma."

The early stages of turning the mind toward the dharma can sometimes be accompanied by fear and uncertainty as our deep habit of self-attachment tries its best to get us to go back to how we used to be. I have heard students express fear of giving up on the identity they have spent a lifetime building up in samsara. After all, the different aspects of our identity are what keep us embroiled in samsara. They help us to get recognition and attention. We use these identities to feel self-assured and self-confident, to protect ourselves, and to advocate for ourselves to get what we want. All of these are expressions of our attachment to samsara.

It is difficult to divest the energy that we habitually put into our sense of self. As ordinary beings, we have a great amount of attachment to knowing who we are and using outside people and situations to solidify that sense of self so that it seems dependable, reliable, and permanent. What is the real situation, though? If we take the time to investigate the nature of our own body and mind, we cannot find a single aspect of the self that is permanent. This identity that we have built up is just a facade, just an expression of self-attachment we have been using to help us feel like there's nothing to lose, neither now nor in the future.

It is only through developing renunciation and certainty that the nature of samsara is suffering that we can begin to give up our efforts at continually trying to prove that our identity and sense of self truly exist. If we recognize that we have been playing the role of a magician all along—someone who takes something that isn't real and tries to make it look real—then there is no reason to keep up with the charade. If we begin to truly understand that it is our self-attachment and the habit of working in our own self-interest that has been the cause of our suffering all along, we may also begin to develop the courage and willingness to give it up.

Returning our attention to the remainder of the third line—if you are attached to self-interest, you do not have bodhicitta—Sakya Drakpa Gyaltsen points us to taking up the bodhisattva path (training the mind in bodhicitta) as the very method to do away with self-interest completely. The third line presents a scenario in which the practitioner has given up on self-interest or is at least in the process of trying to do so, so that they are able to work at generating authentic bodhicitta. We might wonder, then, how does this transformation take place?

Focusing on our own self-interest and trying to protect ourselves from having to experience unwanted things are the overwhelming tendencies of beings living in samsara. We work in our own self-interest because we believe it will bring us happiness. Even though this is contrary to our actual experience, we continue in the same way we always have because of the deep attachment we feel to the nature of samsara. It is only beings who have turned away from samsara and outright reject the way that ordinary beings try to find happiness who have the thought and courage to do things differently.

Once the mind takes hold of renunciation, we begin to muster a kind of newfound courage. We might think things like, "I don't care how long it takes or how many times I fail, I refuse to follow the same habits that always cause me to suffer." Armed with this way of thinking, we can begin to turn away from self-interest and enter the bodhisattva path. We shouldn't downplay the power of these newly emerging thoughts. Simply having a glimmer of courage can be like a spark that sets fire to our whole practice, if we cultivate this state of mind and renew our courage regularly.

One of my lamas, a great master named Tulku Dakyong Rolpai Dorje, often said, "You fall down hundreds of times, but every time you fall down, you have to pick yourself back up." This is the great courage we need to kindle in order to practice the dharma authentically. What is the real support for this courage? Our courage can rest firmly on the ground of bodhicitta. Bodhicitta is an incredibly powerful state of mind that is able to bear even the greatest weight and cut through even the deepest selfish habits. We need not worry that there is something inside of us that is too much for bodhicitta to handle. There is nothing that can't be transformed. Some of us may worry that inside we are so full of negativity and darkness that it can never be made light. But this isn't the case. Bodhicitta can purify everything—just as the meaning of the word suggests.

The Diamond-Hard Quality of Bodhicitta

In *Way of the Bodhisattva*, the great master Shantideva said,

> Virtue, thus, is weak; and always
> Evil is of great and overwhelming strength.
> Except for perfect bodhicitta,
> What other virtue is there that can lay it low?*

It may seem contrary to the way we have been thinking until now that all of our selfish and harmful tendencies and all of our negative qualities can be purified by bodhicitta. But if we think about it carefully, it makes sense. All our nonvirtuous conduct comes from selfishness. Because we want happiness for ourselves, or wish to protect and shield ourselves from unhappiness, we generate anger, desire, ignorance, jealousy, and pride. These five poisonous emotions are the cause of harm to ourselves and others. Their very root is self-interest, and their poisonous nature is the essence of self-attachment. As Shantideva points out, no matter how strong our selfish tendencies are, and no matter how great our mistakes were or how much harm we have caused, there is still a chance to turn it around. This is because bodhicitta strikes at and scrapes away at our self-interest until it is completely gone.

Although bodhicitta is often presented in the relative as a series of gradual and conceptual practices where we make others' needs and happiness more important than our own, here it

---

* Shantideva, *The Way of the Bodhisattva*, trans. Padmakara Translation Group (Boston: Shambhala, 2008), 52.

is also being presented as an expression of authentic realization. After all, to have done away with self-attachment and self-interest completely is not something an ordinary being can do. The gem of perfect bodhicitta could only describe a high level of realization. It expresses true freedom from self-attachment or the realization we call liberation from samsara.

Bodhicitta versus Self-Interested Love

When we train in bodhicitta, we are not giving up loving others. In fact, it is just the opposite. We are trying to see others more clearly—to see what they want and need and to try to put them before us. It is important to realize that the attachment we ordinarily identify with as love is not the same thing as altruistic love. That kind of attachment is better understood as self-interested love.

Self-interested love is what we feel when we try to use external people and situations to make ourselves feel better. The problem with this is if we are using someone or something to make ourselves feel better, we have no opportunity to love and care about that person or thing. The connection we have with them is based on how we feel, what we need, and what we want. Our energy isn't focused on them at all. It is tied up in trying to get them to be a certain way or to do something for us. This self-interested feeling is what we are trying to give up when we train in bodhicitta with our loved ones, family, and friends, as we attempt to use these close relationships to learn how to express love more purely and less selfishly.

In the best-case scenario, as we train in bodhicitta, we begin to see through our own self-interested love. As we notice the way that we use others to make ourselves feel better, pushing them to meet our expectations and punishing them in a variety of ways when they don't, the difference between this selfish love and altruistic love becomes more and more apparent. If we become aware of our self-centeredness long enough, it becomes hard to even think that we really care about others. We may become acutely aware that everything we do is because we want someone to treat us a certain way, speak to us a certain way, see us a certain way, and so on. Even if we wish to be a loving and caring parent, spouse, child, or friend, when love is mixed with self-interest, there simply isn't room in our heart for anyone else. We are too full of ourselves.

With self-interested love, similar to the way we use people, we also use external situations to try to make ourselves feel better. We are unwilling to see and accept the world for how it actually is. We view the world in a certain way to make it fit in with what we believe to be true. The moment that we let our guard down and see samsara for what it is, it is incredibly disappointing. Just like the people in our lives, the world isn't going to bring us any lasting happiness or make us feel better.

Once we recognize that we have been expressing self-interested love all along, we have the chance to begin to cultivate bodhicitta. After we see the mistake we have been making, we have the opportunity to start fresh. It is not easy to turn the mind away from attachment and give up on the hopes we have placed on people and situations around us, but finally we can try to find a way to live in the world the way it is instead of pretending the world is different than it is. This is only possible because of the support of bodhicitta, which gives us the strength of mind to begin to see the true source of happiness is found in working toward others' well-being.

The Necessity of Bodhicitta

In the *Aspiration to Generate Bodhicitta, Utterly Pure and Supreme*, Patrul Rinpoche said,

With it, I have what's needed to attain enlightenment.
Without it, there is no method to accomplish buddhahood.
The unmistaken seed for accomplishing supreme
    enlightenment—
May I give rise to bodhicitta, utterly pure and supreme.

This verse points out the necessity of training in bodhicitta as our main practice. Whenever we generate bodhicitta, we refocus the mind on the true purpose of practicing the dharma—to benefit others and do away with the habit of self-interest entirely. Our self-interest takes on many forms and has many guises. It can be difficult to recognize when we are honestly wishing and working for another's benefit and when we are pretending to work for another's benefit but are really angling for ourselves. Also, sometimes our motivation is mixed. We both wish to help another while also wishing to get something for ourselves. If we train in bodhicitta over a long period of time, we can begin to clear up this kind of mixed motivation, which is partly altruistic and partly selfish.

When we generate aspirational bodhicitta, there are two purposes. The first purpose is to relieve the suffering of all sentient beings temporarily. We wish to relieve whatever suffering they are currently experiencing directly or indirectly, in whatever way we are able. The second purpose is to ultimately relieve their suffering. We wish to place them in the state of enlightenment, which is completely beyond the reach of samsara. Once they have been placed in the state of enlightenment, they will never again fall back into the state of temporary suffering.

When we generate bodhicitta, our mind is focused solely on others—their suffering, their temporary relief, and their future happiness. There is no mention anywhere of self-interest or self-benefit.

This brings up an interesting point about how we teach the dharma to modern practitioners and how we should train and practice. In modern times, many people with interest in the dharma find the two purposes of bodhicitta outlined above quite frightening. After all, nowhere in this practice is there any mention of our own suffering! Often students will ask me, "If I spend all of my time focusing on the suffering of others and trying to relieve their pain, what will happen to me?" This way of thinking shows that we have not understood the essence of bodhicitta and how the dharma works. Also, if we think in this way, we may find that we are unwilling to cultivate bodhicitta because we may feel excluded from the happiness that we wish could be experienced by others. We may also find it difficult to give rise to a mind full of joy and warmth that wishes genuine happiness to others. However, this way of thinking is not taught in the dharma; it sounds more like the Western idea of martyrdom getting mixed in with the dharma. But we need not fear—bodhicitta brings happiness to everyone, including ourselves, by its very nature.

Training in bodhicitta is a radical idea. It goes completely against our ordinary way of thinking. Ordinarily we think of ourselves first and put ourselves and our own interest at the forefront. But here we are being told to do exactly the opposite. We should put others' interests first and put them at the forefront. At the same time, we should step out of the way and do our best to serve them. Only something this radical could undo and do away with the intense suffering we all experience moment by moment.

Be Cautious of Some Modern Practice Instructions

I have encountered a style of teaching bodhicitta to modern practitioners that tries to incorporate the struggle modern practitioners have to put others first. This kind of teaching directs us to cultivate bodhicitta for ourselves rather for than others and to use ourselves as the object of mind training—for example, in the practice of *tonglen*. Many modern students train in this way and find it helpful in dealing with some painful aspects of their personality, such as self-hatred. I certainly support any practitioner who is trying to do away with a strong and destructive emotional tendency such as self-hatred. But while this type of training may be effective in assisting practitioners dealing with an intensely negative state of mind, it diverges from the method of training in bodhicitta set out by the lineage masters. We should understand the difference between using this kind of method to work with a strong emotion, such as self-hatred, and the methods to train in bodhicitta that are taught according to the lineage by the lineage masters.

According to the lineage masters, bodhicitta does not include any wish to benefit us, nor does it consider our own self-interest. If it did, it would directly contradict the third line of Sakya Drakpa Gyaltsen's quotation, "If you are attached to self-interest, you do not have bodhicitta." When we train in bodhicitta, we do not use ourselves as a direct or principal focus. We also do not worry about ourselves or think about what will happen to us when we train in the mind of bodhicitta. If we engage in any of these thoughts, we move the mind away from its actual focus during practice—which is on benefiting others. If we do not fully place our focus on others and the wish for their happiness, there is no way for the mind to cut through its own self-obsession. After all, if we use ourselves as the object of the practice, we have never turned our attention away from ourselves at all.

Please do not misunderstand the clarification that I am giving. Just because we don't focus on ourselves when we train in the mind of bodhicitta does not mean that the practice of bodhicitta doesn't help us. Training the mind in bodhicitta enables us to cut through self-attachment *because* we drop the habit of being self-centered and self-interested. Once the mind cuts through its own self-centeredness, we start to feel better. It is such a relief to take a break from our own suffering. This is the way suffering is: the more we look at it, the more we think about it, the more we talk about it, the more we play it out in our mind, the stronger it gets. And as soon as we turn our focus away from that suffering, we begin to relax. After we engage in this kind of mind training for a period, we may notice some good qualities that we didn't realize were there—such as greater peace of mind, fewer strong emotions, less sensitivity, and more patience. If we have already started training in the mind of bodhicitta, we know what a sense of relief it can bring. As our self-attachment decreases, our own well-being naturally increases.

Temporary and Ultimate Happiness

When we train in bodhicitta, our suffering diminishes both temporarily and ultimately. Our suffering diminishes temporarily because when we focus on others, we give rise to a wholly virtuous state of mind. This is logical. Virtuous causes give rise to virtuous results. Also, when we help others, we feel good—it feels good to do good things for others. Focusing on others is also a very effective way of not focusing so much on our own suffering. It is important that we examine these benefits of training in bodhicitta. We should ask ourselves if we experience some of these positive results in our own mind. If so, we will probably feel inspired to train harder and be less frightened to give up focusing on ourselves and our own needs.

When it comes to our dharma practice, we shouldn't take someone else's word for it. We should always apply the teachings personally and take them to the level of experience we currently have. For example, in this case, we can examine the different results of different states of mind. How does it feel to be angry, competitive, or selfish? And on the other hand, how does it feel to feel empathy or compassion? When we step outside of ourselves and extend kindness, warmth, or love to others, do we experience the feeling or joy or relaxation that the teachings talk about? We should make a thorough examination of the benefits of training in an altruistic mind so that we can be inspired to cultivate it more and more.

Additionally, the teachings say that the benefits of training in the mind of bodhicitta go far beyond this moment, this year, or even this lifetime. We Tibetans have a saying, which is that when someone trains in the mind of bodhicitta, their life will move "from happiness to happiness." This wonderful saying refers to the self-compounding nature of joy and happiness when we cultivate bodhicitta. We will be happier tomorrow than we are today; happier next year than we are this year; happier when we are older than when we were young; and happier in our future lifetimes than we were this lifetime. This is the power of bodhicitta— we experience increasing happiness now and in the future both because of our loving and joyful state of mind at present and because, in the course of our mind training, we accumulate virtuous karma that then ripens as future happiness. Even though many unwanted situations will occur in our lives because of negative karma we have accrued in the past, we will have more patience to face them. We will settle down and find the ground of renunciation, and instead of getting emotionally involved in unwanted situations, we will be able to maintain our focus on others and how to best bring them happiness.

The second purpose of bodhicitta, that of placing sentient beings in the state of ultimate happiness, also indirectly ensures we will also benefit. Only a realized buddha or bodhisattva would have the ability to directly benefit another sentient being or relieve their suffering. When we make the aspiration to place sentient beings in this state, we are also making an indirect commitment to accomplishing our own realization. However, even though we should understand this truth as a practitioner, it should never be the focus of our practice. This indirect benefit to ourselves is just part of the magic of bodhicitta. We never have to make any kind of selfish wish for ourselves or make sure we were included in the scope of our practice. We never have to hope for our own realization. It will naturally happen because realization is the result of training in bodhicitta. We can have confidence that we don't have to worry about ourselves. As long as we truly love and dedicate ourselves to others, we will have everything we need.

How Do We Begin Generating Bodhicitta?

If we follow the words of Patrul Rinpoche, the great nirmanakaya emanation* of Shantideva, our mind training is sure to have a genuine result. Patrul Rinpoche advised that whenever we cultivate bodhicitta, we should accompany our practice with the prayer that we will one day be able to give rise to perfect bodhicitta, free of any blemishes of self-attachment. Then, focusing on the two purposes of bodhicitta, we can give rise to the wish to relieve the suffering of all sentient beings and to ultimately place them in the state of enlightenment. In the beginning, this can feel intellectual or rote. We may not feel any warmth or blessings at all when we generate bodhicitta. But we shouldn't minimize our efforts. Even having a sincere wish and warm feelings toward all sentient beings is a good place to start.

We can also start to reflect on bodhicitta in our daily lives. How often do we remember this altruistic mind during the day? How often do we give up on this compassionate state of mind because of selfish emotions such as anger, desire, jealousy, and so on? It is good to review our thoughts and behavior so that we can start to notice if we are really stepping on the path of genuine dharma and applying the meaning of bodhicitta to ourselves or not. If we are not applying the lojong teachings, it shows that we are forgetting the dharma. If we are not thinking about benefiting others, the dharma we are practicing isn't genuine.

---

* Patrul Rinpoche is said to be a future incarnation of Shantideva—a nirmanakaya, or embodiment of a wisdom being in human form.

We Tibetans have a saying: "Don't focus on the words, focus on the meaning. Don't focus on yourself, focus on the dharma." "Don't focus on the words" means don't get caught up in superficial things. Don't intellectualize everything. We should apply the meaning, make sure we practice properly, and hone our experience. If our intention is to practice the path of dharma, we should make sure we don't step off the path by failing to apply the teachings to ourselves.

"Focus on the meaning" means that we should examine whether the meaning of the dharma is dawning within us. Did we recognize the authentic meaning of the teachings—did we extract its very essence? Is that essence taking root inside of us?

"Don't focus on yourself, focus on the dharma" means we should not put so much focus and attention on our outer appearance as a dharma practitioner. In other words, we don't need to worry if we look like a dharma practitioner on the outside. If we focus on the dharma instead, we can transform from the inside out so that eventually we fully embody the dharma. Lama Tsepel is an excellent example of someone who cut through his own self-attachment and was able to embody the genuine dharma through and through.

It can also be helpful to look at our behavior in hindsight and see if what we do, say, and think show that we are focusing on the meaning of the dharma. In the beginning, when we have a lot of self-attachment, we may have a lot of confusion about how to apply the dharma. This is because the instructions of the lojong teachings are difficult to comprehend. It is hard to believe that finding happiness is as simple as giving up on self-interest and working for others' happiness. Also, it is difficult to curb our negative personality traits in the beginning, so when we try to apply the dharma, our best efforts can get mixed up with some of the habits we already have that make it difficult to get along with others. As a result, when we try to apply the lojong teachings, we might later realize we have gone about it in the wrong way.

It is especially important not to apply the lojong teachings or use the practice as a way to feel superior to others or to belittle others' struggles and suffering. When applied correctly, the lojong teachings increase the qualities of compassion, tolerance, and empathy for others, and do not fuel ordinary habitual tendencies such as judgment, criticism, or feelings of self-righteousness. In hindsight, it often becomes clear that we make mistakes when we are emotionally invested in a certain outcome. When the mind is full of emotions and self-attachment, it is difficult to see clearly and even more difficult to control our actions.

For example, we may know that we should hold our tongue and not speak out in anger, but if we can't handle our emotions in the moment, we may say something we shouldn't and have to deal with the fallout later. In these times, if we are able to calm ourselves down, renew our aspiration to practice the dharma, and focus on our wish to bring happiness to others, we may be able to make a different decision. For example, we may decide not to say anything at that moment and instead wait to express ourselves at a different time, when we can speak deliberately rather than lashing out. Whenever we are able to pacify our emotions and feelings of strong self-attachment, we can have more confidence that our actions will match the intention that we have to practice the dharma.

One easy way to understand this is when we look at someone else, we can see the difference between their skillful conduct and their errors, but when it comes to ourselves, it is much more difficult to see. It is easy to see the other person clearly because we aren't experiencing that person's emotional investment. We are just looking at them from the outside. In the same way, if we can begin to pacify our strong emotions by applying the lojong teachings, we can see ourselves and the situations we face more objectively, which will enable us to act much more skillfully.

How Confusion Begins to Clear Up

When we look at samsara, it seems straightforward and objective until we realize that it's an expression of our own mind. Samsara is colored by our perception, our emotional investment, our attachment, our wanting things to be a certain way, and our wanting to avoid certain things. According to the dharma, we see our own confusion all the time. In fact, it may be all we see! Because of self-attachment, there is no way to see clearly. It is only when we cut through self-attachment that our vision becomes more accurate and genuine. We are finally able to see past our own ideas, confusion, and superimpositions—our own karmic perception.

Our habitual ideas and perception are just like a hamster wheel. We are trapped inside this wheel, constantly running and giving momentum to our habits. In the beginning, bodhicitta is like a sharp axe that we can use to jam the gears of the hamster wheel. But as we train at a higher level, we can use this sharp axe to cut through the very root of these habits and excavate the root of samsara. As our practice advances, it is also possible to cut through our confusion and all of the obstacles to the path of dharma. Once we can see with less confusion and less self-attachment, it becomes possible to apply the genuine dharma a little bit more.

Since the source of our experience of samsara is self-attachment, as we cut through the root of that self-attachment, we see samsara a little bit more nakedly, the way it actually is. The more we experience the nature of samsara and its suffering, the more desire we have to escape it, and the more capacity we have to apply the dharma. This is the natural progression toward being able to enter the path of dharma and remain on it free of obstacles and pitfalls.

The Fourth Line

If you are attached to this life, you are not a dharma practitioner.
If you are attached to samsara, you do not have renunciation.
If you are attached to self-interest, you do not have bodhicitta.
If any grasping is present, it is not the view.

A Language-Based Commentary on the Fourth Attachment

The fourth line states, "If any grasping is present, it is not the view." Here, "the view" refers to the view of meditation. Even though we may have read a lot of books about the dharma or even attended dharma teachings, we may never have encountered the phrase "the view." This phrase has a very specific meaning. At the ultimate level, "the view" refers to wisdom itself. But we need to exercise patience if we wish to gain an understanding of wisdom's ultimate nature. After all, it is something that is beyond the sphere and activity of the ordinary mind. Wisdom can be described as an inseparable appearance and emptiness that is beyond all partiality and limitations, and beyond verbal description and conceptual thought. We will explore what that means throughout this section.

In the Vajrayana teachings, the understanding of the view of meditation is not only extremely precise but also essential to our progress on the path. After all, if we do not understand the view of meditation, even if we train in certain practices that have brought realization to the lineage masters of old, how can those same practices result in realization now? They cannot, because they do not share the same fundamental basis, or view, of the great masters.

The great lojong master Atisha said, "Because the view is incorrect, you have not realized the genuine meaning." Atisha points out that when we begin with an improper, imprecise, or mistaken view, it is impossible to gain authentic realization. Therefore, it is essential to take the time to come to a correct understanding of and to correct our mistaken ideas about the nature of the view of meditation and ultimate wisdom. Otherwise, when we try to train in the view, our practice is just going to reinforce the same habits we have now, and they are sure to bring us even more suffering in the future. If we think in this way, we can see why Sakya Drakpa Gyaltsen included instruction on the view of meditation as the pinnacle of his four-line presentation of the path.

Some of us may have gained some understanding of the view of meditation by reading texts or receiving teachings on emptiness or the *prajnaparamita*, also called the paramita (perfection) of wisdom. But we should know that the nature of the view is a topic that scholars and yogis alike traditionally study in depth for years, decades, or even their whole lives. Without receiving the proper guidance, teaching, and training on this subject, our understanding of this profound topic may be vague or incomplete. If our understanding of the view is shallow and remains on the surface, it cannot support a genuine Vajrayana practice. Therefore, it is imperative that we dedicate ourselves to listening to and contemplating teachings about the view of meditation as presented by the Vajrayana tradition, because this is the only way that we can develop a basis for practical engagement and experience.

The View of Meditation versus Our Ordinary Perspective

The word translated as "view" in the original Tibetan is *ta wa* (Tib. *blta ba*). But both in scripture as well as everyday conversation, *ta wa* has a variety of uses. *Ta wa* can mean "point of view or perspective." When used as a verb, it can also simply mean "to see." These additional uses of the word point out some of the most important features of the phrase "the view." The view is the way that we see things. It is also our own perspective or point of view. These meanings point out that the ordinary meaning of the word *view* is tied to our own perception and is always personal to us.

But as many of us know, our own perception can be trouble-some. It is often influenced by strong emotions, memories, thought patterns, and habits that we know cause us to make mistakes and perpetuate our own suffering. For example, we know we shouldn't do something. Even before we do it, we realize it's going to turn out badly. But pushed by an impulse rooted in a strong emotion or idea, we do it anyway. And after we do it, it turns out badly, just like we knew it would. We knew better, but we did it anyway. This happens not just once in our lives but over and over again.

Many of us have been trying all kinds of things to overcome these strong thoughts, feelings, and impulses so that we can be more balanced, grounded, and reasonable. For that reason, Western culture has come to rely on the idea of objectivity. In this very scientifically driven culture, objectivity seems to offer us shelter from our strong emotional impulses. If we can be objective, we may be able to put aside our repetitive thoughts and strong emotions and make decisions based on sound judgment. After all, science is based on fact, not emotion. If we could embrace an objective, scientific way of seeing things, it might almost seem possible to escape the trap of our own minds and emotions.

Because Western culture does not have a deep tradition that defines the nature of wisdom and shows the path to realize its nature in the way that Buddhism does, *objectivity* has come to hold a meaning similar to *wisdom* for many Western people. Some might go so far as to think of it as being similar to the limitless altruism of the lojong masters, since objectivity seems to offer the ability to put oneself aside and make scientific decisions free from selfish interference. But according to Vajrayana Buddhism, no matter how hard we try to put aside our emotions, tame our thinking, or undo our deep habits, objectivity is impossible. Even more importantly, achieving even a high level of objectivity is not the same thing as realizing the nature of wisdom, according to the Vajrayana.

If we were to equate wisdom to objectivity, we might mistakenly think that realization is something easily achieved. For example, I have heard realization described as "constant improvement" by some new age renderings of the dharma. But this idea could never be congruent with wisdom itself, which is a state of equality that is vast and even, beyond any movement, change or improvement.

Viewing wisdom as something that is easily achieved has only one result. We trick ourselves into thinking that we do not need to go through the hardship of following the path of lojong from the very beginning until we reach the pinnacle. Instead, we can follow the ways of pop culture, psychology, and new age spiritual techniques, which are much easier since we do not have to give up our self-attachment in order to put these into practice. We can focus on becoming more objective, discerning, self-aware, and emotionally intelligent, and try to give up the many biases we observe in ourselves. Of course, there will be some benefit to these efforts—we will no doubt become more balanced and skillful in handling some situations. But cutting through the very root of samsara's suffering takes more than the mind's effort—it takes the incisive sword of wisdom.

According to the Vajrayana and especially the Middle Way teachings, the view of meditation is something completely different from our personal perspective or view. This is because our perspective always presents a bias no matter how hard we try to overcome it. This bias is the sum of our past karma, experiences, habits, emotional patterns, and beliefs. Even if we are more emotionally stable, balanced, or grounded, we never truly give up that perspective and identity of "I." Therefore, the Vajrayana always presents the ordinary mind and its way of seeing as being subjective. The objectivity that many of us try to achieve isn't possible.

Asserting the problem with objectivity is not unique to Buddhism. Science itself has proven that objectivity doesn't exist. For example, particle physicists have shown that the design of an experiment always influences the outcome. The design of the experiment, we could say, carries the perspective or point of view of the scientist who designed it. So, two experiments meant to measure the same thing can come out with different outcomes. This seems so contrary to the idea of science, which appeals to so many of us because it seems impartial, unemotional, and outside the realm of subjectivity. If even science cannot achieve objectivity, it seems logical that human beings are even less likely to be able to achieve it.

Rather than trying to minimize our thoughts and emotions to downplay their influence, as practitioners, our time would be better spent examining how *unobjective* we actually are. Our thoughts and emotions constantly influence our perception. Have you ever noticed that you may experience the same words or situation differently depending on your state of mind? For example, if you are upset or angry and someone tells a joke, you might not get it, you might feel angry with the person telling the joke, or you might even feel annoyed by others' laughter. But if you are in a good mood, lacking heavy or agitated energy, and you hear the same joke, you might laugh. This simple example shows the mind's subjectivity. We are highly changeable, and how we see things depends on the different influences present in the mind. Even if those emotions, memories, habits, or preferences are very subtle, they are still there. Being balanced and grounded cannot get rid of them.

The Meaning of "Grasping"

The other essential word in the line is "grasping." According to the Buddhist teachings, grasping is the primary defining influence in the mind. Grasping is an innate habit. The Madhyamika teachings assert, "First I grasp at I, and then I grasp at mine." As we have mentioned, self-grasping is the very cause of our identity, our perspective, and all of our self-cherishing. Therefore, it is also the cause of all our ignorance and suffering. Because self-grasping is the basis for having the perspective and point of view of "I," it makes sense to say that this same grasping is what obscures the nature of wisdom. After all, the moment our view and experience are tinged with the perspective of "who I am," it cannot be the nature of wisdom. Grasping itself negates the possibility of wisdom. In other words, when grasping is present, the view of meditation simply becomes the view of self—or better yet, a selfish view.

Eradicating this view of self, the presence of identity and self-perception, is extremely difficult and requires tenacious and proper application of the teachings. It cannot be achieved by something as simple as "emptying the mind" or "not thinking about anything." According to the Buddhist teachings, our sense of self, emotions, habits, and thoughts must be purified for the mind to be free of them. As we purify the mind more and more, wisdom dawns. This brings us back to the first three lines of Sakya Drakpa Gyaltsen's teaching. It is only by following the steps outlined by these lines that we become a practitioner who can truly cut through and purify self-grasping such that we can begin to catch a glimpse of wisdom—which has been there all along but has been hidden by the mind's thick overlays of self-attachment and ignorance.

Clarification on Grasping by the Mahasiddha Tilopa
The mahasiddha Tilopa said to his student Naropa,

Son, appearances don't bind.
Grasping binds.
Therefore, cut through all grasping.

In this quotation, Tilopa clarifies the meaning of "grasping" set out in Sakya Drakpa Gyaltsen's fourth line. Here, "binds" refers to the strong grasping and attachment we have to the appearances of the self and the entirety of the phenomenal world and beings—the nature of samsara. Remember how the second line of Sakya Drakpa Gyaltsen's quotation stressed the necessity of renunciation toward the nature of samsara? Renunciation supports the kindling of wisdom because once we have true renunciation, we see the futility of grasping and generating attachment to the nature of samsara and all of its activities, which only brings us misery. Tilopa takes this idea even further and reveals the more radical idea of how to directly engage with wisdom.

Tilopa points out to his heart son Naropa that the five desirable objects of the senses—form, smell, sound, taste, and touch—do not actually bind us to samsara. Not only do they not bind us to samsara but, because we grasp at them, they cause us suffering. This way of thinking is the basis for the profound practices included at the level of Atiyoga Dzogchen, such as self-liberating appearances. Like the meaning conveyed by Tilopa's words, this style of practice directly cuts through all of the mind's grasping.

As lojong practitioners, we can prepare ourselves to be proper vessels for this level of teaching by training ourselves to reduce the mind's grasping toward internal and external appearances. It is extremely helpful to reflect on the advice given in the great lojong texts such as Way of the Bodhisattva, where Shantideva asserts,

> Scorn and hostile words,
> And comments that I do not like to hear—
> My body is not harmed by them.
> What reason do you have, O mind, for your resentment?[*]

---

[*] Shantideva, The Way of the Bodhisattva, trans. Padmakara Translation Group (Boston: Shambhala, 2008), 141.

What harm is caused by someone speaking to us in an angry or disrespectful manner? As Shantideva points out, the sound of the words, and the words themselves, do not cause us any physical harm. However, when someone says something we do not want to hear, we immediately grasp it and generate a strong emotion based on hearing the sounds. Even though the sound itself is neutral, because of the mind's grasping, we generate afflicted states of mind such as resentment, arrogance, indignation, or anger. Or if someone happens to say something we like, because of the mind habit of grasping, we generate afflicted states of mind such as craving, desire, pride, or attachment. From the point of view of a practitioner who is trying to apply wisdom to their practice, our suffering is not caused by the person speaking or what they say at all. It is caused by the strong emotion generated after the mind grasps at sound as an object of the senses.

That is why Tilopa points out that it is actually the mind's grasping at internal and external appearances that binds us to the suffering of samsara. This is an essential thing to understand if we want to follow the path of lojong to its pinnacle and then apply the profound teachings of Atiyoga Dzogchen or Mahamudra, which provide the means to actualize the mind's own nature of wisdom.

It is important that we think more about the nature of internal and external appearances. If these myriad appearances are capable of binding us to samsara, what is the point of training in bodhicitta, meditation, and traditional methods of purification? In other words, if our suffering is caused by all of the things we see, hear, smell, taste, and touch, as well as the concepts and emotions that arise in conjunction without grasping at those sensory objects, the suffering of samsara will never end. After all, we have no control over the appearances of the world around us. Most of us have tried to assert control over life situations and circumstances and find ourselves powerless to do so.

Buddhism presents a different way to relate to the suffering we experience. It teaches that the source of this suffering is our own mind rather than being caused by someone or something. This is good news for spiritual practitioners. If the problem lies with the mind's grasping, that is something we can change. But we should also realize that actualizing wisdom is deeper than just a change of attitude or seeing things in a different light. It is not just optimism. To truly transcend suffering, we must do what the lineage masters who came before us have done—we have to cut through the mind's innate habit of grasping at everything.

How do we do this? If we apply what is presented in the first three lines of the teachings as well as mind training, we will gradually reduce the mind's grasping. Even when we only reduce the mind's grasping a little bit, we still feel a great sense of relief. When we grasp less often at thoughts and feelings, as well as the details of everyday life, we are more relaxed, less distracted, less agitated, and have more capacity for joy. In our daily life, we may experience more patience, argue less, or speak more tolerantly. Although this is not the same as realizing the nature of wisdom, on a very practical level, this is the way we reduce our own suffering as well as the suffering of others.

Grasping and Fixation

In the Buddhist teachings, the words *fixation* and *grasping* are used to describe the way the mind grasps at internal and external appearances. *Fixation* describes the mind's grasping at sensory objects that appear on the outside. We could say that our apprehension of form, our recognition of sound, the sensation of taste, and so on are all the mind's fixation on external objects. Essentially our entire experience of the phenomenal world is nothing more than the uninterrupted display of the five desirable objects of the senses. We can see here the basic problem with the idea of objectivity—how can our perception of the five desirable objects of the senses be objective when perception itself is the uninterrupted display of the mind's grasping and fixation?

The other way the mind works is by *grasping*, which refers to the mind's attachment to inner phenomena—emotions, thoughts, habits, internal discourse, distraction, and so on. Similarly, how could our personal emotions, thoughts, internal discourse, and so on be objective? We may not have thought about it in this way before, but grasping and fixation constantly interact. They strengthen and reinforce each other. When we fixate on how something appears externally, whether we like it or dislike it, we generate thoughts and emotions on the inside, which then are grasped at by the mind. These thoughts and emotions then influence how we see the outer phenomenal world. For example, if we hear the loud sound of a fire alarm and feel startled and upset, then we carry that feeling of being startled and upset with us and are more likely to interpret subsequent situations as being negative or upsetting. As we fixate and grasp on inner and outer appearances, we generate more thoughts, more emotions, and more karma. This entire cycle is put into motion by grasping. When we reflect in this way, we can see why Tilopa's advice is so insightful and crucial. By cutting through the mind's grasping at any moment, we can interrupt this cycle.

From the point of view of a realized master like Tilopa, these outer and inner positive, negative, and neutral appearances of the mind don't cause us any problems. It is only our grasping and fixation on their appearances that cause us to generate strong emotions and to suffer. This is evident when we consider the simple example that something that brings us unhappiness may not make another person unhappy. We may be served a meal that is meant to please us, but we think it tastes awful, whereas the person sitting next to us thinks the same meal is delicious. Both of us apprehend the appearance of the same meal, but due to the mind's grasping and fixation, we experience it differently. The experience is not determined by the appearance of the meal itself but rather the grasping and subsequent reaction we have toward its taste.

We may wonder which is better—to like the meal or to dislike it? According to the way ordinary people think, it seems more positive to like the meal. It is good to appreciate what others do for us, and more positive to have a good thought than a bad one. However, according to Tilopa, whether we liked the meal or disliked it, both reactions are a form of grasping that binds us to the nature of samsara and its suffering. That is because in both cases, we generate karma based on the mind's grasping and attachment, and the habit of grasping and fixation toward the outer and inner phenomena of samsara strengthens. In one case, we have grasping and fixation toward a taste we don't like. In the other case, we have grasping and fixation toward a taste we do like. Both are expressions of the mind's subjectivity, and because our perspective is imbued with grasping, it accumulates karma that binds us to samsara.

Many practitioners tend to oversimplify what it means to give up grasping, attachment, and preferences and embody the view of meditation. It seems like we could give up the mind's grasping by embracing objectivity, trying to put aside our strong feelings, habits, and preferences. But the mind's innate grasping is extremely deep and deceptive. We grasp without knowing we are grasping. We bind ourselves to samsara without knowing that we are involving ourselves in the cycle of suffering. Without truly understanding the view of meditation, and using the techniques and methods to actualize that, there is no way to rely upon the ordinary mind to self-discover the nature of wisdom. In fact, this is contrary to the words of realized masters such as Patrul Rinpoche, who asserted, "The view is completely beyond ordinary mind."

The Futility of Grasping and Fixation

The pandita Shantipuri said,

> All phenomena, the objects of the mind's fixation, have
> never existed.
> Without a doubt, neither has the mind that grasps or
> confusion.

Shantipuri gives us more insight into the nature of wisdom, as well as the futility of grasping and fixation. As he asserts, nothing and no one truly exists in the entirety of the phenomenal world. The Buddhist teachings describe all appearances of beings and phenomena, including the self, as being of the nature of an illusion, a mirage, or a rainbow. They have no essential or substantial nature. They are impermanent, compounded, and will decay or pass away in time. Therefore, the Vajrayana teachings assert that all beings and phenomena appear in just the way we believe they do, yet they do not truly exist in the way that we believe they do.

Beings and phenomena appear to be lasting, unchanging, permanent, and real, but their nature is fleeting and insubstantial, just like a rainbow. We describe their nature as both interdependent and empty. "Interdependent" means that they arise based on the convergence of many causes and conditions on a moment-by-moment basis—causes and conditions that depend on each other. This is like the nature of a rainbow, which only appears based on the conditions of water particles in the air, sunlight, the proper environment, the proper atmospheric conditions, and so on. This same rainbow is fleeting—if these conditions do not come together, or one is suddenly absent, it will not appear. According to the Vajrayana teachings, everything dependently arises, even the self that we cherish so much.

The nature of dependent arising even applies to the realization of wisdom. As practitioners on the Vajrayana path, we must gather together all the causes and conditions for the realization of wisdom and the actualization of enlightenment. If even one of these causes and conditions isn't present, realization will not dawn.

The word *interdependent* contrasts with the word *independent*, which is the way we ordinarily think about the nature of the self and phenomena. Independence implies that something stands on its own and that it has an essential and permanent nature—that is, a soul or a spirit. Reflecting on the interdependent, impermanent, and insubstantial nature of everything is a powerful tool for taming the mind's grasping. After all, what is the point in grasping at and becoming pleased or upset by internal and external appearances when neither ourselves, the act of grasping, nor the thing we are grasping at have any substantial nature? As Shantideva explained in *Way of the Bodhisattva*,

> All things, then, depend on other things,
> And these likewise depend; they are not independent.
> Knowing this, we will not be annoyed
> At things that are like magical appearances.*

Although we may recognize the truth in Shantideva's words, it is another thing entirely to tame the mind and its tendency to grasp so that we are no longer witnessing and participating in the mind's elaborate drama.

Emptiness and Interdependence

Emptiness and interdependence, or dependent arising, are like two sides of the same hand. They always go together because anything arisen from causes and conditions must be empty.

---

* Shantideva, *The Way of the Bodhisattva*, trans. Padmakara Translation Group (Boston: Shambhala, 2008), 135.

"Emptiness" is a very literal translation from the original Tibetan, *stongpa nyid*, and it means "empty of truly existent nature." Upon examination, we see the logic that self and all phenomena arise dependently because they only appear due to the coming together of causes and conditions. Since anything arisen from causes and conditions is free of a truly existent nature, anything dependently arisen is empty—and thus anything that is empty must also be dependently arisen.

The metaphor of the two sides of the same hand points out the inseparability of these two natures. First, it asserts that emptiness is dependent arising. What is the logical consequence if something is not dependently arisen? Something not arisen from causes and conditions must have a truly existent nature—since that thing is independently established and must come into being due to its permanent, essential nature. Then also the display of dependent arising is emptiness. Just like the rainbow that appears due to causes and conditions coming together, a rainbow's apparent nature is vivid, fleeting, and free of any truly existent nature whatsoever.

Although many of us may have had the impression that the nature of wisdom is emptiness, according to the Madhyamika teachings, we cannot define the nature of wisdom solely as the nature of emptiness. Rather, emptiness must be qualified by its inseparable complement of appearance, which is also the display of dependent arising. Therefore, the Madhyamika teachings state that the nature of wisdom is indivisible appearance and emptiness.

It is helpful to consider a few additional points to better understand the nature of emptiness. Emptiness is free of assertions—for example, "this is like this" or "that is like that." Why is this so? Because emptiness arises on a moment-by-moment basis, it must be free of any extremes, such as existing or not existing. Ultimately it cannot be asserted that phenomena have any particular color, shape, size, and so on. If this were the case, phenomena would be tinged by some truly existent, essential nature.

Of course, when we are discussing the way phenomena appear as opposed to their ultimate nature, they appear to exist, remain, and pass away. They have defining qualities such as color, shape, size, and so on. But again, this display of appearance is dependent on other factors. An appearance dawns because the proper causes and conditions have come together. When those causes and conditions do not converge, the appearance will not display. That is why we say that the self and phenomena are at once both dependently arisen and empty. They appear in just the way we think they do, but they do not truly exist in the way we believe they do.

If neither the self nor phenomena exist, why do we suffer? As Tilopa points out, it is because of the mind's innate habit of grasping. When we grasp at the self, sensory objects, beings, and phenomena as though they truly exist, we ourselves create the momentum to continue experiencing the suffering of samsara.

The Application of Emptiness to the Self

When we consider the nature of dependent arising, it becomes obvious that while the self appears, it is empty and does not truly exist. We can look back on our life using memories and photographs to document our physical development. We can think back over our shifting beliefs, emotions, and changes in personality. We may have fallen in and out of love, had deep friendships that changed over time, and experienced the illness and death of loved ones. When we think in this way, it is obvious that "I" is not permanent. But still, inside we feel there is some lasting, permanent, essential nature called "I." This is the deceptive nature of self-grasping. We have been grasping at the identity and our sense of self for so long that even in the face of knowing that we are impermanent and dependently arisen, we still cannot feel, believe, or act as though this is true.

Perhaps if we make a close examination of the body—recognizing it as a heap of constituent parts such as tissue, blood, bones, fluids, tendons, and muscles—we can more easily recognize that even we are formed by the coming together of causes and conditions. However, it is difficult to turn this intellectual exercise into a genuine feeling of certainty that the nature of "I" must be empty. This shows the necessity of training in the lojong tradition as the basis for realizing the nature of wisdom. Many of us may want to skip the foundational contemplations and practices included in the first three lines of Sakya Drakpa Gyaltsen's verse and go straight to resting in the view of meditation. However, this is not the way the Vajrayana path has been practiced and realized by the lineage masters. Our grasping at the nature of samsara—at everything we think, feel, see, smell, taste, hear, and touch—is so strong that merely thinking that the nature of "I" is empty cannot cut through our steadfast belief. We must gradually cut through this grasping at "I" by applying the advice of the masters—beginning with sending the cares of this life from the mind, developing toward samsara, training in conventional bodhicitta, and so on. In that way, we can reach the level of a Vajrayana practitioner who is ready to directly apply wisdom.

Just as we are the nature of emptiness and appearance, this is also true of other sentient beings and phenomena. The five desirable objects of the senses, to which the mind fixates, all share the nature of appearance and emptiness. This is also true of the mind, our loved ones, friends, and enemies. It makes sense to ask ourselves, "What is the point of grasping onto myself, other beings, and phenomena as though they are going to last forever? What is the use in generating anger, attachment, jealousy, greed, or arrogance toward something that has no truly existent nature and is bound to change at any moment?" Grasping and fixating upon beings and phenomena that are transient like a rainbow is futile. It only brings suffering and loss.

Gampopa's Fourth Dharma

Grant your blessing so that my mind may turn toward the dharma.
Grant your blessing so that dharma may progress along the path.
Grant your blessing so that the path may clarify confusion.
Grant your blessing so that confusion may dawn as wisdom.

The fourth line of Gampopa's *Four Dharmas* states, "Grant your blessing so that confusion may dawn as wisdom." What is necessary for confusion to dawn as wisdom? First, Gampopa's words point out that it is not easy to become a practitioner for whom confusion dawns as wisdom. We should make heartfelt prayers and aspirations that we will be able to realize the nature of wisdom and thereby place all sentient beings in the state of enlightenment, free from suffering. Also, it is helpful to note that, similar to Sakya Drakpa Gyaltsen's fourth line, Gampopa's fourth line also presents the pinnacle of the path. To actualize its profound meaning, we need to enter the path of dharma and follow the path from beginning to end so that we can reach this stage, where catching a glimpse of wisdom is possible. If we follow the path in the manner of the lineage masters, we will build the proper foundation and become a proper vessel to engage in the more profound practices of the Vajrayana.

Once we have built the proper foundation, we also need a deep and unmistaken understanding of the view of meditation, which was defined above as indivisible appearance and emptiness, free of any partiality or extremes. In other words, the view of meditation must be beyond ordinary mind, our personal point of view, and our biased way of seeing. It cannot be limited by the mind's grasping in any way. If the view is mistaken, even if we follow the practices taken up by the lineage masters, confusion cannot dawn as wisdom.

To refine our understanding of the view, we need to rely on the path of lojong to cut through our strong grasping at the self and the display of the phenomenal world. Otherwise, the view of meditation will easily be tinged by our own ordinary view and perspective. Whether we are a beginner or longtime Buddhist practitioner, if we work at training the mind, and then we receive a direct and profound instruction like the one given by the mahasiddha Tilopa, we will be ready to apply it.

Other preparation is needed to be able to transform the nature of confusion to wisdom. We need to engage in not only the practices presented on the path of lojong but also special Vajrayana lineage practices that can help us to purify the mind deeply, and we need to make a vast accumulation of merit. I would encourage you to catch your emotions rather than just identifying with them or pursuing them. If we try to do this on a regular basis, we can develop the skill and awareness of recognizing when emotions are arising. When we recognize this, we may also be able to use different techniques to reduce or cut through the mind's grasping. A lot of mindfulness and introspection is needed to support this.

While it is important to follow the path of lojong to its pinnacle and then apply pointing-out instructions, it is necessary to do so under the guidance of a qualified lineage master. Because of the mind's fixation on outer sensory objects, we are confused. Likewise, because of the mind's tendency to grasp, we are confused. Because of these deep habits of grasping and fixation, our confusion is uninterrupted and causes us to perpetually circle in samsara. Like samsara itself, the suffering we experience is uninterrupted and limitless. How do we interrupt the stream of confusion and suffering? Again, this can only be done by cutting through the mind's grasping.

Once we have gained intellectual certainty in the view of meditation, we need to take it to the level of experience. In other words, we need to practice. We can only gain personal experience of the nature of wisdom through trying to rest in its nature often and over a long period of time. Meditation carries us to the state of experience, and that experience carries us to the state where confusion begins to dawn as wisdom. This is the state where whatever appears and whatever movement occurs internally is nothing more than the good condition for confusion to dawn as wisdom. If we cut through the mind's grasping, then the same appearances that cause us suffering right now will become a supportive condition for gaining more experience and realization of the nature of wisdom.

If we really cut through the mind's grasping at internal and external appearances, no matter where we are and what we are doing, the external world is not going to affect us in the ordinary way. It will simply become the positive circumstance for our own wisdom to increase. And all of our internal mental and emotional activity will not agitate us such that we engage in the endless cycle of creating more and more afflictive emotions. Where will this take us? We will be able to dedicate ourselves to acting wholly in the best interest of others because we will no longer be restricted by our self-attachment, for example, by having hesitation or doubt such as, "If I help this person right now, what will happen to me?" This is the real path to enlightenment. If we follow the path step by step, it is within our reach.

A Meaning-Based Commentary on the Fourth Attachment

To fully understand the meaning of the fourth line of Sakya Drakpa Gyaltsen's quotation, it is helpful to closely read the third and fourth lines together and see how the meaning of the fourth line builds upon the third, as well as the lines that came before. In the third line, the crucial point is developing authentic bodhicitta that is free of any self-interest. It is helpful to notice that, like the fourth line, the main idea of this line is cutting through the mind's grasping—toward the self and our own benefit or happiness. To cut through our self-interest, we train the mind in making others equal to or more important than ourselves, thereby diminishing the mind's grasping even more.

Cutting through the mind's grasping is also the main topic of the first two lines. In the first line, we turn the mind away from ordinary life and toward the dharma. Taking time to train in the four thoughts that turn the mind toward the dharma is essential when we enter the path, because the grasping human beings have toward ordinary life is so overwhelming that it is difficult to even begin to practice the dharma. Based on the foundational practices, we gain confidence in the path of dharma and the reasons to practice dharma so that we can cut through the mind's grasping of our thoughts, ideas, and beliefs about life and the way that life should be. Based on this training, we become less invested in ordinary life, and we can begin to put more time and energy into the dharma.

After entering the path and making some headway in turning the mind toward the dharma, we face another large obstacle also fueled by the mind's grasping. From beginningless time until now, we have been circling in samsara based on our grasping at the belief that it is possible to find happiness in samsara. As we tried to find happiness in samsara, we grasped at and generated attachment toward loved ones and dislike, resentment, or hatred for those we found undeserving; made wishes for wealth and material success; wished for things to go the way we wanted and for them not turn out the way we didn't want; wished for things not to change; made the wish to remain healthy; made the wish to avoid illness and death, and so on. We grasped at all these hopes and were also tormented by fear, as we knew in our gut that it was unlikely for any of these wishes to come true. Therefore, the advice in the second line is to cut through the mind's grasping at the nature of samsara, as well as the belief that samsara can bring us happiness.

To truly cut through the mind's grasping at the nature of samsara, we must reevaluate how we have been doing everything.

We must apply the path of lojong in a radical manner so that we can begin to turn all our ideas and habits upside down in order to reverse and purify them. That brings us to the third line, where we face yet another layer of the mind's grasping—this time the root of all grasping—self-grasping, or self-attachment. We must train in lojong very tenaciously to dig up the deep root of self-cherishing, as it colors and contaminates our feelings, thoughts, and actions. The habit of self-grasping is innate and subtle. Self-grasping or grasping toward our perspective or way of seeing makes it extremely difficult to achieve the view of meditation, which is beyond all partiality and bias. Even if we make some progress in training in bodhicitta, if we are unable to give up our personal identity of "I" completely, we will not be able to properly recognize the view of meditation. As practitioners on the path of lojong, we must push ourselves to give up even the subtlest expressions of self-grasping based on the practices of conventional bodhicitta.

Based on training in conventional bodhicitta as taught in the third line, we are prepared to train in the nature of wisdom—also called ultimate bodhicitta—in the fourth line. Ultimate bodhicitta is bodhicitta's wisdom aspect, the fruition of having trained in and perfected conventional bodhicitta. This term is used to describe the nature of wisdom in the general Mahayana and also the Madhyamika teachings as I have defined them above.

However, when the term *ultimate bodhicitta* describes the nature of wisdom according to Atiyoga Dzogchen, it has a special definition. When we discuss it at this level, ultimate bodhicitta comprises three qualities. Like the Madhyamika view, ultimate bodhicitta, according to the teachings of Atiyoga Dzogchen, has both empty and apparent qualities. These are called the empty essence and clear nature. However, ultimate bodhicitta contains the third quality of all-pervasive compassion. It is particularly helpful to reflect on the inclusion of all-pervasive compassion as it relates to Sakya Drakpa Gyaltsen's fourth line. For compassion to pervade everywhere, to be the view completely free of partiality and limitations, the mind must be free of any grasping toward anyone or anything. We must have cut through grasping at even its subtlest level through the repeated application of the teachings on conventional bodhicitta.

Some Practical Advice

Conventional bodhicitta seems so ordinary that we may wonder if it is really possible that training in lojong can lead us to the pinnacle of the path. The Kadampa masters of old, who perfected the practice of lojong, as well as masters of all four lineages of Vajrayana Buddhism who followed, showed us that this is certainly the case. These four lines from *Parting from the Four Attachments* simplify the process for us. All the suffering we experience in this lifetime is caused by grasping and attachment to the self—nothing else. All the happiness that can be experienced originates in having positive thoughts and wishes to benefit others. What we truly need is deep, irreversible certainty that sees that the nature of samsara is suffering. We also need to know that we are the creator of all the suffering that we experience—no one else creates it; it is the display of our mind, karma, emotions, habits, and so on. Self-attachment is the great creator of ordinary perception and our identity.

To be liberated, the crucial thing we need is renunciation, the turning away from samsara. When we do that, we may not embody the dharma perfectly, but we no longer think or act how we used to. We may be more open to practicing the dharma and less afraid of changing and making different choices than others around us. At that point, we can begin training in conventional bodhicitta. In doing so, if we truly work hard, we can learn the skill of letting go of attachment to ordinary life. If we can give up this attachment, there is a real possibility that we will be able to embody the meaning of the fourth line, which is ultimate bodhicitta.

Once we reach the pinnacle of the lojong path, we are fully prepared to receive and practice the teachings of Atiyoga Dzogchen
or Mahamudra. As we recognize and rest in the view of meditation, subtler and subtler layers of grasping fall away. They are
purified and vanish of their own accord. But if we do not follow
Sakya Drakpa Gyaltsen's advice step by step, there is no way to
be properly prepared for this level of practice. We will never be a
proper vessel to hold these teachings, and if we can't hold them
and digest them, we simply can't understand or practice them.
There's just no way to do it.

We are all wasting so much time. We need to wake up from the
daydream we are living in. We may think we have enough time
to practice and that we are smart enough to gain the realization
of wisdom and transcend the suffering of samsara without much
effort, just as we mastered ordinary knowledge when we were in
school. Or, as Westerners, we may have the idea that we are more
sophisticated and economically better off than others. This feeling
can become part of our identity, such that we become entitled in
our practice of the dharma—we feel we are especially deserving
of profound teachings and that we have a special ability to realize
them. But having this feeling is simply a *mara*, a huge obstacle to
the practice of dharma that will hinder our progress or push us
off the path entirely.

We may think we can avoid training in the practices presented
in the first three lines of *Parting from the Four Attachments* and
still practice Atiyoga Dzogchen or Mahamudra because our intel-
ligence will make up for the practice we haven't done and the
foundation we haven't developed. A lot of Western Buddhists
have approached Vajrayana Buddhism like this, and unfortunately
they have not succeeded. This approach hasn't worked because
it overlooks the biggest obstacle to cutting through the mind's
grasping and actualizing the view of meditation—self-grasping.
Unless we have trained with great tenacity and diligence, we may

be able to generate some feelings of warmth and compassion, but we will not be able to reach even the level of generating bodhicitta, let alone be able to rest in the nature of ultimate bodhicitta—the mind's own nature. It is not possible that we could discover a way to abide in that quality all on our own.

More on Subjectivity

In *Thirty-Seven Practices of a Bodhisattva*, Gyalse Thogme Zangpo elucidated the proper way that bodhisattvas—masters of the lojong lineage—relate to appearances, grasping, and the nature of ultimate bodhicitta:

> Whatever appears is your own mind.
> From the very beginning, your mind has been free of
>   fabricated extremes.
> Knowing this, not holding onto dualistic grasping and
>   fixation
> Is the practice of bodhisattvas.

This verse explains that all appearances are expressions of our own mind. This statement completely goes against any notion of objectivity. Instead, it asserts that everything we perceive, whether it be internal or external, is an expression of the mind. Understanding that the nature of internal appearances is subjective is easier, since our thoughts, concepts, ideas, and habits obviously arise from our mind and cannot be factual or objective. However, don't take my word for it; it is important that we each examine this for ourselves.

Everything that appears to the mind internally is deeply connected to and the expression of our own conceptual mind. Even if we try to put aside strong thoughts and feelings, subtle thoughts, emotions, and habits are still there. We may have noticed this when we tried to work with our emotions in the past. Even though we put them aside and try to move past them, they come back when we least expect it, and we often realize that we haven't let go of things we thought we had dealt with long ago. Sometimes our efforts at letting go of past situations and emotional experiences is referred to as "peeling the onion." Peeling the onion is considered progress in our spiritual and emotional development, according to many people. But according to the Vajrayana, we can keep peeling the onion in perpetuity and will never get to the core. Our strong habit of grasping cannot just be set aside by will. It always comes back to haunt us because it is grasped tightly by the mind. It must be completely purified so that, in the words of Gampopa, confusion can dawn as wisdom.

Maybe it makes sense to think that internal appearances—our internal world—is subjective, but it seems like a much bigger stretch to say that outer appearances are also subjective. Most ordinary people will not accept this to be true. Aren't the appearances of beings and the phenomenal world real? How can they be expressions of the mind? Again, don't accept it just because I say it's true. It is important that each of us examines it for ourselves. The Vajrayana teachings assert that outer appearances are not objective because we experience these appearances as the five desirable objects of the senses based on the mind's object fixation. Here, the word *desirable* is the key. Because we grasp at and generate attachment (positive, negative, or neutral) to the five objects of the senses, our perception of these objects of the senses cannot be objective—that is, beyond the influence of personal thoughts, feelings, and opinions. As soon as the mind grasps at these appearances and generates any kind of attachment—even neutrality—they can no longer be considered objective. Based on grasping, appearances become "mine," something personal to the perceiver. It is impossible for the perception of these appearances, which are subject to the mind's dualistic grasping and fixation, to be objective.

Even if others see the same appearance, they see that appearance based on their own view, perspective, and way of seeing. Although human beings have shared karma that causes them to see appearances of the world similarly, when they perceive those appearances, it is based on the grasping of their own mind. Even in the most balanced of cases—where my grasping is neutral and someone else's grasping is neutral—still, we are not seeing the same appearances objectively nor is it guaranteed that we are seeing things the same way.

This is something that is often shown by a recounting of Buddha Shakyamuni's first turning of the wheel of dharma. The story goes that when the Buddha Shakyamuni gave teachings at Sarnath in Varanasi, eighteen different students heard those teachings in eighteen different ways and wrote them down as the basis for Buddhist practice. These teachings then became the basis for different sects of Buddhist teachings. So, even in the case of listening to the dharma, we hear things differently, perceive things differently, and interpret them differently. This story shows that even the mere perception of sound, one of the five desirable objects of the senses, is subjective—it is individual and particular to us. For that reason, Gyalse Thogme Zangpo's first line says that "whatever appears is your own mind."

How does this impact us as practitioners? It reminds us that we should not get too invested in appearances—taking them too seriously, causing us to have emotional reactions that are too strong. We lojong practitioners training in wisdom should always remember that we see things according to our own karma, habits, emotional patterns, and so on. In other words, what we see is a projection of the mind or we are seeing through the lens of the mind. As ordinary beings who have not realized the nature of wisdom, we cannot see without this lens, which is created by the mind's grasping.

If we wish to purify our impure vision, the only way to do so is to apply the lojong teachings, which can help us further cut through the mind's grasping toward the self as well as internal and external appearances. In other words, the perceiving (grasping) mind is always arising in conjunction with the object to fixate upon. However, it is possible for this impure display to transform based on the practice of meditation, especially according to the tradition of Atiyoga Dzogchen.

If mind's impurities—its emotional and cognitive obscurations and habitual tendencies—were all exhausted and purified, we would no longer be a perceiver who is perceiving internal and external appearances. In fact, all aspects of impure appearance would dissolve just like mist in the sky. And so this grasping and fixation at beings and objects—including our self and the entire phenomenal world; and dualistic constructs like good and bad, purity, and impurity—all comes from the mind.

The second line of this verse from Gyalse Thogme Zangpo states that from the beginning, the mind has been free of "fabricated extremes." The nature of the mind free of any obscurations is the buddha nature. In other words, from the very beginning, the mind has been the nature of wisdom, which is free of any limitations, extremes, or the conceptual mind's workings. This original buddha nature must be free of fabrication, superimposition, overlay, and obscuration. The mind's own ultimate nature is free from all these mental constructs and conceptual activity.

In Vajrayana tradition, the one who is able to realize this does so through the threefold activity of understanding, experience, and realization. Understanding comes from listening to teachings many times and engaging with them on a personal level—for example, through contemplation. Experience is based on application of the teachings, as well as personal guidance by a qualified lama. The connection between lama and student is one of the special features of the Vajrayana tradition (and the lineage of Atiyoga Dzogchen) because the lama is the only one who truly carries the living lineage and lineage blessings. Without the lineage blessings, the teachings remain dead, no matter how much we try to put them into practice. Therefore, realization can only occur when the qualified student makes the proper connection with a qualified lama and receives the lineage blessings, transmission, and upadesha directly from that master.

Based on this threefold activity of understanding, experience, and realization, whoever is able to see this vast and even state of mind, beyond all partiality, limitations, and extremes, will see the nature of ultimate bodhicitta. When we are able to see ultimate bodhicitta, all grasping and fixation will dissolve like snow falling on the surface of a lake.

The third line begins with the phrase "knowing this." Knowing this points out that we need to use the intellectual mind to determine the nature of appearances and the mind's ultimate nature. But our knowing must go beyond the level of mere intellectual knowledge. Instead, we need to have examined these ideas so thoroughly that we have come to a deep determination and certainty that their nature is as we discussed above. Then, to take this determination even further, we apply the teachings—we train in them and practice them—so that we can purify our impure perception and begin to approach the genuine experience of ultimate bodhicitta.

We practice by making an effort not to take internal and external appearances so seriously—after all, they are subjective and not an objective reality. For example, when the mind is caught up in ideas, we recognize, "Oh, that's a thought" or "That's an emotion," and we do our best not to pursue it or put more energy into it. By not putting much energy into it, we purify that thought or emotion at a certain level. However, when we are inexperienced, we will not be able to truly cut through the mind's grasping from the root. We should go back to our practice of lojong and work with an antidote we are familiar with to try to calm and pacify our own response. For example, if someone made us angry, we could first recognize that it's an emotion that arose because of our own self-attachment. To dampen the emotion, we could also generate conventional bodhicitta by reflecting on that person's suffering and difficulties. Purification occurs when we train in this way over a long period of time. Even if thoughts and emotions keep coming up, if we don't pursue them, and then apply antidotes, our mind gradually begins to release its habit of strong grasping. This helps us to get closer to the level of a real bodhisattva who doesn't grasp or fixate upon anything. In other words, they see the actual view of meditation, free of the partiality and limitations imposed by the grasping of the ordinary mind.

The Key Point of the Mahayana Vehicle

As practitioners of the Mahayana, we should know that the pith meaning of the entire Mahayana condenses into this single verse by Gyalse Thogme Zangpo, which describes the way a bodhisattva comes to rest in the nature of ultimate bodhicitta. Once we understand the way that a bodhisattva recognizes and increases the experience of wisdom, as well as the way they train as they ascend the *bhumis** and paths, enlightenment becomes possible. This is because we can truly see what the nature of wisdom is and what the realization of that nature might be like—rather than just having a vague idea of it or thinking it is like being extremely intelligent or knowledgeable.

Nyaglab Pema Dadul, a yogi who attained the incredible accomplishment of Atiyoga Dzogchen called rainbow body, where the body itself dissolves at the time of death and only the hair and fingernails are left, gave instructions on how to traverse the bhumis and paths toward the state of enlightenment. He said, "Free of grasping, free of method, rest directly in the nature of suchness."

---

* *Bhumis* are the stages of spiritual development and realization of a Buddhist practitioner.

Here, the key word is "directly"—resting directly in empty appearances, free of any overlay, superimpositions, grasping, or conceptual aspect of a method. There is no mental construct of perceived, perceiver, and act of perception. As long as the mind is still engaged in grasping at subject/object duality, viewing appearances as being outer objects rather than subjective expressions, direct resting is impossible. If we still believe that internal and external appearances are objective and real rather than transient, interdependent, and the mind's own expression, we will not find the way to go beyond the limitations of the mind's grasping and the application of a method or technique.

The Way to Train in Wisdom

The *Prajnaparamita Sutra* states,

> Thoroughly knowing the way that all phenomena are
>   unborn and empty
> Is the supreme engagement in the nature of wisdom.

This quotation points out that determining the nature of phenomena as apparent emptiness, and resting in that empty, unborn nature, is the way to train in the nature of wisdom. Wisdom, indivisible appearance and emptiness are free of grasping, free of establishing one position and refuting another, free of accepting and rejecting, and free of assertions. Also, when we rest in the state of wisdom, it is said to be like the nature of space. Space is nondual because it cannot be divided into this and that. It has no directions or limits. It is vast and even. However, this is just a metaphor. This metaphor focuses on wisdom's empty quality; however, we should never fall into the extreme of emptiness alone. Emptiness is never separate from appearance; we only know that phenomena are empty because we see their dependently arisen nature.

These lines from the *Prajnaparamita Sutra* also point out how essential it is to determine what emptiness is, and to make that knowledge deep and thorough. All apparent phenomena are empty—including our own internal appearances, as well as the external appearances of the world and beings. We can ascertain that apparent phenomena are empty because they arise interdependently. Whatever arises based on causes and conditions lacks any truly existent nature whatsoever. These lines also state that phenomena are "unborn." Phenomena are described as "unborn" because the concept of *birth* refers to a truly existent thing coming into being. This description doesn't make sense. If a baby took birth and its nature was truly existent, it could never grow, mature, or pass away. Change would be impossible, and in fact, even the appearance of taking birth would be impossible.

We can ask ourselves how something that truly exists comes into being. Again, an existent entity must exist in perpetuity. Since it exists, it must have been the way it is from the very beginning and continue on that way forever. Therefore, this state of permanence cannot describe "birth." In Madhyamika philosophy as well as the Vajrayana, we say that phenomena are unborn, because they dependently arise on a moment-by-moment basis. This description captures the fleeting and impermanent nature of everything.

Having worked through the teachings in the first three lines of Sakya Drakpa Gyaltsen's quotation as described herein, we have made some progress on the Vajrayana path. At this point, we may be starting to notice that our thoughts, feelings, and actions are out of touch with our Buddhist ideas and contemplations, as well as the lojong practices we have been applying. Although we may have accepted the idea that the self, the outer world, and all apparent phenomena are empty, we may not act like it. We may still get just as emotionally involved in our thoughts and emotions as we used to. This is a common experience. If we are a serious practitioner of the dharma, or we want to be, this is something we should take time to reflect on. If we notice this is true about ourselves, we should ask ourselves, "Why am I getting so involved in grasping at all of these appearances, which are merely an expression of my own confusion?" This is an excellent question for all practitioners to investigate.

If we have had the experience of realizing that we do not actually see or act in congruence with our spiritual practice, we can probably relate to how frustrating it is. For example, has anything like this ever happened to you? You are having lunch with some friends and get annoyed with them because they are talking about something that you think is unimportant and not worth your time. You might feel annoyed before you can even think about the dharma, and that annoyance is accompanied by feelings of irritation and thoughts like, "Why are my friends being so annoying right now?"

Even though we try to take up the path of lojong, we may not have a single thought that the one who is annoyed is actually *me* and that annoyance is actually caused by *my* mind's own grasping at the sound of them talking and what they are saying, as well as *my* emotional expectations of our time together. Later, we might think back in hindsight and realize we could have applied the lojong teachings in that moment—we could have applied Shantideva's advice not to grasp at and attach to sound, or we could have reflected on sound's empty nature. But our habit of grasping at appearances and then placing blame on outer conditions for our own unhappy state of mind is a very deep habit that is difficult to reverse.

One way that we can work with this kind of situation is to reflect more on the nature of appearance and emptiness. Everything that appears is empty, and likewise, emptiness can appear in an unlimited variety of ways. Still, we must train in reflecting on the nature of appearance and emptiness for a long time to be able to remember it when the mind is afflicted.

We may wonder why we grasp at phenomena if they are empty. The way in which conceptual mind comes into being has to do with our grasping at what is called the three conceptual spheres. First, we grasp at the self, the one perceiving the appearance. This self-grasping is the sphere of the subject, or the perceiver. Next, we grasp at the sphere of the object, or the recipient of the action. This object could be a material object—for example, a glass of water. It could also be the recipient of an action, such as a person who is spoken to by another person. Finally, we grasp at the sphere of the action or the interaction between two or more people. An action could be something like giving the glass of water to another person. An interaction would be more like two people having a conversation or hugging. These three conceptual spheres compose anything we could possibly perceive. They are the building blocks of the mind's grasping and fixation, which, in turn, build our dualistic perception. And while all three of these conceptual spheres appear to exist, the nature of them all is empty. In contrast to the three conceptual spheres, Patrul Rinpoche said, "Wisdom is beyond the sphere of the ordinary mind's activity."

Thinking in this way is very different from our ordinary perception. Ordinarily, internal appearances such as thoughts, emotions, and habits—as well as external appearances such as the display of the universe and all beings—appear to us as a complex web of continuous activity all related to me, with "I" firmly in the center. Whenever perception occurs, all appearances become personal to me, and I see them as "mine"—my world, my life, my problems, and so on. However, if we apply the technique of resting in the emptiness of the three spheres to a given situation, we may be able to reduce the mind's grasping or reaction a little bit at a time as we retrain and purify our habit of dualistic perception.

As soon as the mind grasps at the three spheres and perceives something, the mind will also engage in the mental function of imputation. Imputation is the mind's act of labeling and naming, as we develop a more sophisticated concept of whatever is being perceived. Even the imputing mind itself is primordially free of all extremes, limitations, and grasping. This brings us to another quality of wisdom, which Patrul Rinpoche described as "beyond verbal description and conceptual thought." Because wisdom is beyond the three conceptual spheres, it cannot be conceived of or understood by the ordinary mind. And because the three spheres are empty, there is nothing or no one to impute—they are beyond verbal description, labeling, or naming. This is why the lojong masters gave us the example of training in meditation on appearance and emptiness, free of any contrivance or fabrication, without dwelling on any characteristics or attributes.

No apparent phenomena exist apart from being mere mental imputations. Since the imputing mind itself is also beyond arising, dwelling, and ceasing, all phenomena that appear as the perceiver and the perceived also remain as emptiness free from mental activity. When a yogi has gained certainty regarding the natural state in this way, he or she rests undistracted in the state of not mentally engaging in anything at all. The natural state is just the way that it's always been; it was never created and nothing new is occurring now.

Some Concluding Words

Some teachings, though brief, have the ability to impart the entire wisdom of the Vajrayana tradition. *Parting from the Four Attachments* is just that kind of teaching. After exploring the depth of teaching in this short verse, you can truly now see that it wasn't imparted by an ordinary being in human form but was directly offered by the bodhisattva Manjushri to Kunga Nyingpo. It contains everything essential to the Buddhist path; many more layers of meaning, even, than can be included in this brief commentary.

Having accompanied us on such an intimate journey into the words and meaning of *Parting from the Four Attachments*, I hope it can become for you like the bread that nomads carry with them when they herd yak high up in the Himalayas. When nomads leave their tent early in the morning, they tuck a piece of Tibetan bread in the breast of their wool *chuba.** When they get hungry during the day, they take it out and have a bite. Just like that piece of bread, whenever you are hungry to practice the dharma, just take out this simple verse and rekindle your enthusiasm and understanding of the genuine path to liberation.

Cutting through the mind's grasping and attachment is the most difficult challenge you will ever face. But by following the natural progression of each of these four lines, you may be sur-

---

* A *chuba* is a large woolen cloak traditionally worn by Tibetans.

prised to find you are up to the challenge. If you emulate the example of the masters, following in their footsteps step by step as you work at developing the essential qualities of a practitioner, progress on the path of dharma is a certainty. Sooner or later, you will mature into a being with the realization, heart, and ability to benefit others.

May these teachings be an essential support and guide to all who fearlessly wish to walk the path to perfect liberation. May all beings attain perfect enlightenment, free from suffering!

I bow at the feet of my root lama
Supreme sovereign of the bodhisattvas!

If grasping and attachment toward this life aren't reversed,
Then dharma practice will be superficial; there's no benefit.
Therefore, reverse the mind's deep habit of grasping.
May the perfectly pure dharma be accomplished!

If the mind's admiration for phenomenal existence isn't reversed,
You can't be an excellent practitioner of the dharma; there's no
    benefit.
Therefore, continually contemplate the faults of samsara.
May weariness and renunciation naturally develop!

If you don't rely on bodhicitta, the wish to benefit others,
The mind of awakening will be ingenuous; there's no benefit.
Therefore, completely reverse attachment to self-interest.
May supreme bodhicitta arise!

If grasping and fixation don't dissolve into the expanse of
    wisdom,

Realization will be a facade; there's no benefit.
Therefore, cut through all grasping and fixation.
May supreme realization dawn!

Anyen Rinpoche and Allison Choying Zangmo
Denver, Colorado
Summer 2024

About the Authors

Anyen Rinpoche is a recognized tulku of the Longchen Nyingthig lineage within the Nyingma tradition. Born and raised in Amdo, Tibet, he trained extensively in Dzogchen meditation and Buddhist scholarship under his root teacher Kyabje Tsara Dharmakirti Rinpoche. Founder of the Orgyen Khandroling Dharma Center in Denver, Colorado, Anyen Rinpoche is known for his deep spiritual insight and accessible teaching style. He is the author of many books, often in collaboration with his wife and translator, Allison Choying Zangmo, including *Union of Dzogchen and Bodhichitta*, *Stop Biting the Tail You're Chasing*, and *The Tibetan Yoga of Breath*. He is also founder of the Phowa Foundation, which focuses on helping people prepare for a peaceful and conscious death.

Allison Choying Zangmo is Anyen Rinpoche's longtime student, personal translator, and collaborator. She has received extensive Buddhist training, including empowerments and teachings from various prominent Tibetan masters such as Khenchen Tsara Dharmakirti Rinpoche, Tulku Rolpai Dorje, and Denpai Wangchuk. With Anyen Rinpoche's encouragement, she began teaching through the Orgyen Khandroling Dharma Center in Denver, Colorado, in 2017, and now plays a vital role in bringing the dharma to a Western audience. She is coauthor, with Anyen Rinpoche, of *Stop Biting the Tail You're Chasing* and *The Tibetan Yoga of Breath* and has assisted him with many other titles.